Let Your Garden Bring Good Things to You

We can attract a limitless supply of ch'i into our homes by paying attention to the feng shui of our gardens.

—Richard Webster

Whether you own an estate with formal gardens or rent a studio apartment with room for some flowerpots, you can create an environment that invites and fosters ch'i (universal life energy), which in turn attracts happiness, prosperity, and health. The latest release in Richard Webster's *Feng Shui* series for the home and workplace, *Feng Shui in the Garden*, shows beginning and expert gardeners alike how to arrange their gardens to attract this beneficial energy.

Use proven feng shui principles to determine which areas of your garden correspond to love and marriage, family, wealth, and career. Learn how to select the most advantageous location for your garden, as well as the best use of colors, fragrances, herbs, and flowers to create good fortune and abundance in any of these areas.

Find out which five flowers will bring the most benefits and blessings to your household. Ascertain the most favorable placement of fountains, waterfalls, or swimming pools. Discover how to create a secret garden, even if you live in an apartment!

Whatever kind of garden you grow—herb, zen, formal, cottage, courtyard, or mixed—with *Feng Shui in the Garden*, your good fortune will blossom and flourish.

About the Author

Richard Webster was born in New Zealand in 1946, where he still resides. He travels widely every year, lecturing and conducting workshops on psychic subjects around the world. He has written many books, mainly on psychic subjects, and also writes monthly magazine columns.

Richard is married with three children. His family is very supportive of his occupation, but his oldest son, after watching his father's career, has decided to become an accountant.

To Write to the Author

If you wish to contact the author or would like more information about this book, please write to the author in care of Llewellyn Worldwide, and we will forward your request. Both the author and publisher appreciate hearing from you. Llewellyn Worldwide cannot guarantee that every letter written to the author can be answered, but all will be forwarded. Please write to:

Richard Webster
C/o Llewellyn Worldwide
P.O. Box 64383, Dept. K793-5
St. Paul, MN 55164-0383, U.S.A.

Please enclose a self-addressed, stamped envelope for reply, or $1.00 to cover costs. If outside the U.S.A., enclose international postal reply coupon.

FENG
SHUI

in
the
Garden

RICHARD
WEBSTER

1999
Llewellyn Publications
St. Paul, Minnesota 55164-0383
U.S.A.

FIRST EDITION
First Printing, 1999

Book design: Amy Rost
Cover design: Tom Grewe
Interior illustrations: Jeannie Ferguson
Typesetting and editing: Kjersti Monson

Library of Congress Cataloging-in-Publication Data
Webster, Richard, 1946–
    Feng shui in the garden / Richard Webster. —1st ed.
       p. cm.
    Includes bibliographical references (p.   ) and index.
    ISBN 1-56718-793-5
    1. Feng shui gardens. I. Title.
SB454.3.F45W435 1999   99-17821
                         CIP

Llewellyn Publications
A Division of Llewellyn Worldwide, Ltd.
P.O. Box 64383, Dept. K793-5
St. Paul, Minnesota 55164-0383

Printed in the United States of America

Other Books by Richard Webster

Feng Shui for Apartment Living

Feng Shui for the Workplace

101 Feng Shui Tips for the Home

Chinese Numerology

Astral Travel for Beginners

Spirit Guides & Angel Guardians

Aura Reading for Beginners

Seven Secrets to Success

Feng Shui for Beginners

Dowsing for Beginners

Numerology Magic

Omens, Oghams & Oracles

Revealing Hands

Forthcoming in this Series

Feng Shui for Love & Romance

Feng Shui for Success & Happiness

Dedication

For my good friend,
who also happens to be New Zealand's
leading feng shui consultant,
Danny Thorn

Acknowledgments

I would like to express my grateful thanks
to T'ai Lau for his help and advice.

Contents

Introduction

The kiss of the sun for pardon

The songs of the birds for mirth;

You are nearer God's heart in a garden

Than anywhere else on this earth.

—*Traditional*

For many, gardening is almost a spiritual experience. It can be a good way to relax and reduce stress. The pleasure of tending living plants is a motivation, and can even be a form of therapy. Gardeners can produce their own food, or beautify their home with flowers. There are countless reasons to enjoy gardening, and most keen gardeners don't stop to think exactly what it is they enjoy most about their creative interest.

One important aspect is that the garden is our own space; we can do whatever we want within it. On our own property, we have total control and can create virtually anything we wish. Naturally, we are constrained by considerations of space, finances, and the family's needs. Our gardens need to include space for a variety of activities: a place to simply sit and relax; perhaps a place to entertain; maybe somewhere to grow vegetables; and, if you have children, xii **Introduction**

somewhere for them to play. We also need to allow room for such mundane things as clothes lines, trash cans and garden sheds.

From time immemorial, people have enjoyed being close to Mother Nature—the living earth. In the fifteenth century, Marsilio Ficino wrote: "The world lives and breathes, and we can draw its spirit into us."[1]

Gardens provide food for all of the senses—not only food to eat, but colors, textures, shapes, sounds, and scents that we can savor and enjoy. We can arrange them in many different ways to create the effect we want. For instance, I have planted Queen of the Night in every home we have lived in because, for me, the delicate scent is soothing, restful, and brings back happy memories of my childhood. If it wasn't for those memories, it is unlikely that I would have this plant in my garden.

A friend of mine loves the sound of the wind rustling through the leaves of tall trees. Not surprisingly, this has been a feature of every garden he has had. A lady I know encourages songbirds into her garden by providing plenty of berries for them. She is a portrait painter and finds that the song of the birds stimulates her creativity.

Gardening is a wonderful creative outlet that reveals a lot about us. For instance, a garden containing neat paths, manicured lawns and hedges, and formal flower beds without a weed in sight obviously belongs to a different type of person than the more natural garden where everything is allowed to grow and spread as it pleases. However, both gardeners may be devoted to their gardens and spend equal amounts of time working in them.

Gardens mean different things to different people, since we all see the world from our own particular perspective. William Blake knew this when he wrote:

> *The tree which moves some to tears of joy is in the eyes of others only a green thing that stands in the way: as a man is, so he sees.*[2]

For many people, the garden is simply a flower box in a window. However, those people often lavish as much care and attention on their few square feet as other people do on a large garden, and receive the same therapeutic benefit.

The Chinese have been concerned about living in harmony with the earth for thousands of years. From their observation of nature came feng shui, which literally means "wind and water." They believed that if you lived in harmony with the living earth, you would lead a life of contentment, happiness, and abundance. A beautiful Chinese proverb illustrates this:

> *If I keep a green bough in my heart,*
> *the singing bird will come.*

Naturally, this philosophy meant that they paid more attention to the landscape than is usual. The relationship between human and nature has always been of prime importance, and nature is symbolized in the garden. One of the greatest blessings that gardeners have—particularly those who practice feng shui—is that the singing bird is always present.

Although traditional Chinese gardens sometimes seem rather austere to Western eyes, they are designed to provide peace, tranquility and comfort. The aim is to allow the visitor to enter a different world full of beauty and harmony. The approach is different, but Western gardeners have remarkably similar aims when designing their gardens.

The absence of grass is one of the major differences between Western and Eastern gardens. In the East, sand, stone, rocks, and even compacted earth are frequently used. Colored pebbles are often relied on to create attractive mosaics for paved areas. The fact that plants are used sparingly can be another surprise for Westerners.

Eastern gardens are characterized by their use of walls to enclose areas within the garden and to define borders. Frequently, a lattice screen or window allows glimpses of the garden, providing a foretaste of the pleasures to come. The Chinese do not like seeing the entire garden at a glance— walls create an air of surprise and mystery.

In the East, contrasts are of extreme importance. This relates to the concept of yin and yang, which we will discuss later. A large, jagged rock might be placed beside a cool, reflective pond, creating both contrast and balance.

Rocks have always been important in Eastern gardens. They symbolize mountains, which are the home of the Immortals. Rocks can be placed singly or in groups. They provide a perfect focal point for a garden, and are often used for meditation purposes. However, it would be a mistake to assume that Chinese gardens are solely used for rest and contemplation. They are frequently used for social activities as well, and it is a matter of pride to have a beautiful garden where you can entertain.

In ancient China, poets and calligraphers would work in an outdoor pavilion or a room overlooking the garden in order to be at peace with nature and to enhance creativity.[3]

Feng shui is used both indoors and in the garden, though directions are more rigid indoors. Gardens are designed to flow freely within the confines of the walls, which are built according to the basic directions of feng shui. Allowing freedom in the garden emphasizes the difference between being inside and out.

I hope that with the help of this book, you will be able to create and maintain a harmonious feng shui garden that will help you to live a life full of peace, happiness and abundance.

1

What Is Feng Shui?

Feng shui is the art of living in harmony with the earth. Its origins go back at least 5,000 years. At that time, Wu of Hsia, later to become emperor of China, was conducting irrigation work on the Yellow River. One day, a giant tortoise crawled out of the river. This was considered a good omen as, in those days, people believed that gods lived in the shells of turtles and tortoises. However, when they looked more closely at the markings on the shell, Wu's men found that they created a perfect three-by-three magic square. This was considered so auspicious that Wu summoned all the wise men of the day to examine it. From this magic square came feng shui, as well as a variety of divination systems including the I Ching, Chinese astrology, and Chinese numerology.

For the first 2,500 years of its existence, feng shui was primarily concerned with the geography of the landscape. The Chinese noticed that if they sited their homes in the right position, good things would flow effortlessly their way. Conversely, if their homes were badly sited, life was a constant battle against the elements.

They found that the perfect position was to have a south-facing home with hills behind it to protect the inhabitants from cold and harsh winds from the north, and with gently flowing water in front. A house in this position was said to contain an abundance of good *ch'i* (Figure 1A).

Figure 1A: The perfect position for a home

Ch'i

Ch'i is one of the most important factors of feng shui. It is the universal life force that is found in all living things. Anything that is done perfectly creates ch'i. Consequently, a beautiful garden or landscape creates a large amount of ch'i. A gently flowing river or cascading waterfall creates ch'i. An artist making a portrait is also creating ch'i.

Wherever you find an abundance of ch'i, the vegetation looks rich and healthy, the air smells fresh and sweet, and the water is cool and refreshing. No wonder people who live in an environment like this lead lives that are rich in happiness, contentment, and abundance. This also explains why people enjoy spending time in a beautiful garden. They are exposed to an unlimited amount of beneficial ch'i.

In feng shui, we want to attract as much ch'i as possible into the main entrance of our homes. In effect, the main entrance is the mouth of the house. Although some ch'i comes in through the windows and other entrances, by far the bulk of it comes in through the front door.

We can attract a limitless supply of ch'i into our homes by paying attention to the feng shui of our gardens. It may seem hard to believe that something you do for relaxation or pleasure is also creating ch'i, thereby increasing the quality of your life at every level and making you happier and more contented than ever before.

Yin and Yang

Yin and *yang* are opposites that cannot exist without one another. The ancient Taoists never tried to define yin and yang, but delighted in coming up with lists of opposites to illustrate their relationship. Examples are: front and back, tall and short, black and white, male and female, and night and day. None of these things can be defined without their opposite. Without a front, for example, there could be no back.

Yin and yang are usually shown as two tadpole-like shapes inside a circle (Figure 1B). This is the Taoist symbol of the universe, as they believe that everything is composed of yin and yang energy. Inside this symbol, one tadpole is black (yin), with a small dot of white (yang) inside it; the other one is white (yang), with a small dot of black (yin) inside it. The purpose of the dot of the opposite color is to demonstrate that inside yin, there is always a small amount of yang, and inside yang is always a small amount of yin.

Yin and yang do not simply sit quietly together. Each is trying to gain supremacy over the other. Consequently, in any situation, if yin is increasing, yang must be decreasing. However, there is always a point where yin

Figure 1B: Yin and yang

will have reached its maximum, and at that time yang will start to gain strength.

The seasons represent this ebb and flow. Spring marks a time of rebirth, of new energy. Yang starts to rise. This carries on through summer, until yang has done all that it can. Yin starts to grow as fall comes, and reaches its full zenith in winter. Naturally, at the end of winter, yin starts to decrease as yang starts to grow again.

In our gardens, we want a balance of yin and yang. For instance, flat land is said to be too yin. Mountainous land is too yang. The ancient Chinese invented pagodas to create yang in flat (yin) environments. We can create yang by planting trees and bushes, or erecting walls or hedges. You are no doubt familiar with the Japanese zen gardens, where rocks create yang in an otherwise flat (yin) environment.

Conversely, if your property is on a steep slope, you should try to create an area of yin. Friends of mine live on a hillside overlooking the city. It is a glorious position, and the views are incredible. However, their property became much better for them once they created a small flat area where they could place garden seats. Now they can sit outside on pleasant evenings and enjoy the view.

Shars

The ancient Chinese believed that ghosts could travel only in straight lines. This is why, in the East, you frequently find bridges that zig-zag across ornamental lakes. The angles are meant to prevent any ghosts from crossing the bridge.

In practice, *shars* are any straight lines or angles that point directly toward your home. A good example occurs if your home is situated at the head of a T-junction. In this instance, a road would be pointing directly toward your home. This shar is bad enough, but it is even worse if the road points directly toward your front door.

Another common example is when the house next door is situated at an angle to your home. Two walls of this home can create a shar, or poison arrow, that points directly toward your home. Roof lines of neighboring houses are also a common source of shars.

You can have shars inside your own property, as well. If your front path heads in a straight line directly from the road to your front door, it is creating a poison arrow, or shar.

Feng Shui Remedies

Feng shui remedies are used whenever balance and harmony needs to be restored. They can be used to conceal a shar, to provide a balance of yin and yang, and to eliminate the harmful effects of an unusually shaped lot.

Fortunately, there is a remedy for just about everything in feng shui. Shars exist only if you can see them. Consequently, a wall, hedge or row of trees that conceals the road heading directly toward your home effectively eliminates the shar.

It is not so easy to remedy a path heading in a straight line toward your front door. If possible, it would be better to replace it with a gently curving path. If this is not possible, there is an alternative solution: you could hang a pa-kua mirror above your front door.

Pa-kua Mirror

A pa-kua mirror is a small circular mirror in the center of an octagonal-shaped piece of wood. The eight trigrams from the I Ching are placed around the mirror (Figure 1C). In effect, the straight line heading toward the front door is captured in the mirror and sent back to where it came from. Mirrors are generally considered to be yin, or passive. A pa-kua mirror, however, is yang and aggressive because of the eight I Ching trigrams surrounding the circular mirror.

Pa-kua mirrors are the ultimate remedy. However, it is better to use a less dramatic remedy whenever possible, saving the pa-kua mirror for situations that cannot be remedied in any other way.

There are many stories concerning pa-kua mirrors. Probably the most famous is the one concerning Bruce Lee. When he became rich and famous, he moved to Kowloon Tong—an exclusive part of Hong Kong. A feng shui expert advised him to hang a pa-kua mirror from a tree to improve his feng shui. The tree was blown over during a typhoon and the mirror was broken. Bruce Lee neglected to replace it, making his death, according to the people of Hong Kong, inevitable.[1]

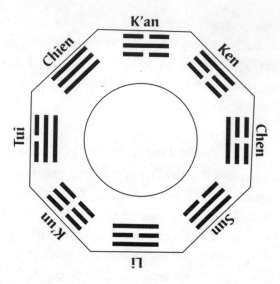

Figure 1C: The eight trigrams of the pa-kua mirror

Mirror wars are common in Hong Kong. Someone looks out of his apartment and sees a shar coming from across the road. He hangs up a pa-kua mirror to remedy the situation. His neighbor from across the road sees this mirror, and puts up one of his own to send the shar back again. The first person puts up another mirror, and in no time at all, each will have hung up about ten mirrors. Finally, the police are called in and order all the mirrors to be taken down.

Trees and Plants

Trees and plants are the most useful remedies for the garden. They can be used to conceal any potential shars from roads, buildings, or anything else that is pointing directly toward your property.

A friend of mine lives in a beautiful home on the edge of a large city. Everything was perfect until a new freeway was built nearby. It passed on one side of his property, and created an angle that looked like a large knife ready to attack his home. In a short period of time, two pets died and his wife became seriously ill.

My friend planted a row of bamboo plants, which effectively made the freeway disappear. Almost immediately, his wife's health was restored and life became smooth and pleasant again. The bamboo also helped eliminate the sounds of traffic on the freeway, in a sense creating a double remedy.

Incidentally, in Southern China, bamboo plants were frequently planted at the back of people's properties as protection. My friend did not know this, but chose bamboo because it is fast growing and provided an effective remedy in a short period of time.

Trees and plants are extremely beneficial because they create an abundance of ch'i. Evergreen trees are considered better than deciduous ones—their green leaves symbolize wealth and abundance. Also, the bare branches of deciduous trees can create shars.

Traditionally, it was considered better feng shui to plant trees behind the house rather than in front of it. This is because houses generally faced south, and trees behind them provided protection from the cold north winds. Obviously, trees are still frequently used as windbreaks. Trees can also conceal anything considered negative or undesirable. For instance, it is considered bad feng shui to overlook a cemetery, church, or police station, as they all create negative ch'i at times. Trees can hide these from view.

In feng shui, all trees are considered to be good, just as long as they are not planted too close to the house. Trees and plants contain large amounts of yin energy. Ideally, they should enhance the yang energy of the sun. If trees are planted too close to the house, they can prevent the yang energy from entering the home, creating an imbalance. *Large* trees can prevent ch'i from entering the home as well.

Trees and plants need to be healthy. They should be removed when they are rotting or dying, as this creates negative, or shar ch'i. It is good feng shui to replace them quickly, as shar ch'i can cause a great deal of harm to the inhabitants.

Incidentally, on a worldwide basis, ten trees are chopped down for every one that is planted.[2] We are losing forty million acres of forests every year—this is more than one acre per second![3] We all have a duty to plant as many trees as possible. By doing this, we are not only creating beauty, we are ensuring the production of oxygen, which trees produce through photosynthesis. Additionally, by planting more trees, we create a limitless supply of beneficial ch'i.

Every now and again, I visit a home where there is no vegetation at all. All plants create ch'i. When we eliminate plants from our lives we deliberately constrict ourselves. This always creates feelings of discontent and dissatisfaction with one's life. In the long run, it can also affect a person's health.

We need flowers and other plants in our lives to create happiness and contentment, as well as good health. Of course, this also explains why we usually take a gift of cut flowers to friends in the hospital.

The relationship between humankind and plants is a complex and subtle one. We need each other, so it is good to have plants indoors as well as out. Indoor plants can add beauty as well as ch'i to our environment. Increasing the amount of ch'i in the home raises the amount of energy we have and makes us feel more vibrant and alive. Consequently, an attractive, healthy plant situated somewhere close to where we study or work can provide pleasure, as well as raise the quality of what we produce. Indoor plants can also be used to conceal interior shars, such as sharp angles.

Water

Water is an effective remedy that almost always creates good feng shui. Water symbolizes wealth and prosperity. However, the water must be clean and preferably moving; stagnant and foul-smelling water creates negative ch'i.

Any water flowing through your property should be in front of the house. Water flowing behind indicates financial opportunities that cannot be properly utilized.

Fish ponds, fountains and swimming pools all create positive ch'i. Kidney-shaped pools should appear to embrace the house (Figure 1D). Pools of this sort become

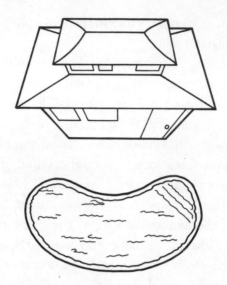

Figure 1D: Kidney-shaped pool

a veritable magnet for money. Pools that face away from the house do the opposite.

Water is an effective remedy when a setting is too yang. This scenario is common in cities, where sometimes all you can see is brick and cement. A fountain or pond in this environment creates a small oasis that is soothing and restful.

Water and plants work very well together, creating an abundance of ch'i. Hong Kong is full of tiny parks, each containing a pond or fountain surrounded by plants. These small green spaces effectively restore the souls of the inhabitants by providing them with peace, tranquility and good ch'i.

Lights

Outdoor lights are extremely effective at alleviating the problems caused by irregular-shaped lots of land. The remedy here is to use three lights: one at each of the two front corners, and the third sited in the middle of the back of the lot.

L-shaped lots can also be rectified. These lots create an angle that sends a shar across part of the property. A light placed at the corner that faces this angle acts as a remedy (Figure 1E). Lights can also rectify problems caused when the house is built well away from the center of the lot. In that case, they help provide balance and harmony.

Narrow driveways restrict ch'i. Lights placed on both sides of the driveway attract ch'i and encourage it to enter.

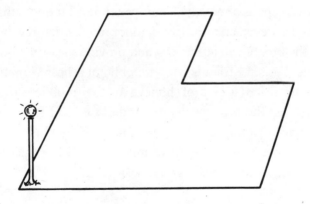

Figure 1E: A light can remedy an L-shaped lot

Sound

Wind chimes create pleasing music in the breeze and remind you that the ch'i is flowing. Wind chimes can be made of a wide variety of materials. Choose chimes that look attractive and sound melodious. These can be placed anywhere, indoors or out. Outside the front or back door are both excellent positions. It is important to be able to both see and hear them.

Other sounds can also create useful remedies. The sound of the breeze rustling in the trees can cover up and eliminate other sounds, such as traffic. The sound of water in a fountain can serve the same purpose and is doubly beneficial, as it is also creating beneficial ch'i.

Movement

Movement as a remedy is more often used indoors than out. However, an attractive outdoor mobile that revolves in the breeze will attract ch'i and provide pleasure to the eyes. We have friends with a mobile of a bear climbing up to reach a pot of honey. As the mobile slowly revolves, the bear gets closer and closer and then falls downward, only to try again. The sight of this determined bear always beings a smile to the faces of people who see it. This creates good, positive ch'i.

The Five Elements

The ancient Chinese believed that everything in the universe was composed of five elements: Wood, Fire, Earth, Metal and Water. Your year of birth determines which of these five elements you belong to. You can find out which one relates to you in the appendix. These elements can be arranged in a number of ways, but the most common are known as the *Cycle of Production* and *Cycle of Destruction*.

The Cycle of Production

In the Cycle of Production (Figure 1F), Wood burns and creates Fire. Fire produces Earth. From the Earth, we obtain Metal. Metal symbolically liquifies and creates Water. Water nurtures and creates Wood.

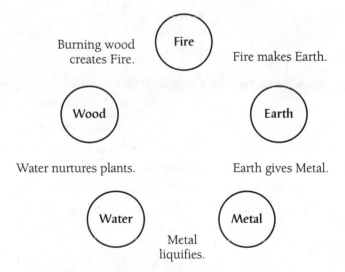

Figure 1F: The Cycle of Production

The Cycle of Destruction

In the Cycle of Destruction (Figure 1G), Wood draws from the Earth. Earth absorbs and blocks Water. Water quenches Fire. Fire melts Metal, and Metal chops Wood.

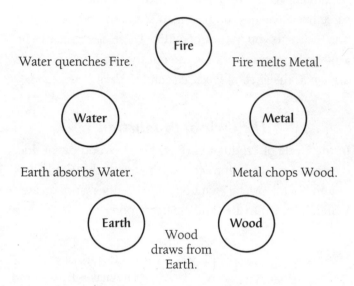

Figure 1G: The Cycle of Destruction

The productive cycle is a highly positive one where each element helps the elements on either side of it in the cycle. The destructive cycle does the opposite, and each element harms the element on either side of it in the cycle. Consequently, if your element is Fire, you would not want too much Water in your garden as Water puts out Fire.

In fact, if you and your partner belong to elements that are next to each other in the destructive cycle, you should check to see what element is between them in the productive cycle, and then make a feature of that particular element in your garden. For instance, if your element was Metal and you were married to someone from the Wood element, you should have something from the Water element in your garden to neutralize the negative aspects of this combination. This is because, in the destructive cycle, Metal chops Wood, but in the productive cycle, Water comes between Metal and Wood.

Naturally, most gardens contain a large amount of Wood, as all plants belong to the Wood element. However, we should also have something in our garden that relates to our personal element, as well as something from the element that precedes ours in the Cycle of Production. For instance, if your element is Metal, you should have something that relates to both Metal and Earth in your garden (Earth precedes Metal in the productive cycle).

Here are some examples of things that could be used in your garden to help you obtain the right balance of your element:

Wood
All plants

Anything that is blue or green

Wooden furniture

Wooden fences

Tall, oblong, rectangular shapes such as poles,
posts, pillars and columns

Fire

Outdoor lights

Candles and incense

Barbecues

Anything that is red

Household pets and other animals

Statues

Anything triangular or pyramid-like in shape

Buildings with sloping roofs

Earth

Pottery, porcelain and ceramic objects

Anything made of clay, brick, tile, marble or adobe

Anything that is yellow or brown

Sand, rocks, stones and crystals

Anything square or rectangular in shape

Metal

Metal furniture

Other metal objects, such as brass pots and
wrought-iron railings

Anything white or metallic in color

Anything that is semi-circular, circular,
arched, or oval

Water

Anything containing water, such as
a pond, fountain or stream

Mirrors and glassware

Anything that is blue or black

Wave-like or curving shapes

Many items are a mixture of more than one element. A square-shaped, metal table that is painted red would be a combination of Earth, Metal and Fire. This would be a good item to place in a garden that consisted largely of grass, plants, and a wooden deck—all of which come from the Wood element. What we are looking for is balance and harmony. By working with the five elements, we can create a garden that complements the personal elements of the people who live in the home, reflects their personalities, and creates an abundance of beneficial ch'i.

In the next chapter we will look at the mystical pakua, and then we will learn how to make practical use of this information in our own garden.

2

The Mystical Pa-kua

In chapter 1, we mentioned the magic square found on the markings of a tortoise shell some 5,000 years ago. This find marked the beginning of feng shui, and the magic square is just as useful today as it ever has been.

Each of the nine boxes inside the magic square relates to different areas of life, and together they comprise the pa-kua (Figure 2A). Using basic feng shui principles, we are able to progress in any of these areas by activating the ones we want.

The pa-kua is placed over a plan of your lot with the bottom of the square (Knowledge, Career, and Mentors) aligned with the main entrance to your property. It can also be placed over smaller areas of land. For instance, you might want to place a pa-kua over your back garden, or perhaps just a small, private part of your garden. In feng shui, this is known as using the Aspirations of the pa-kua.

Wealth	Fame	Marriage
4	9	2
Family	Good Luck Center	Children
3	5	7
Knowledge	Career	Mentors
8	1	6

Figure 2A: The Aspirations of the pa-kua

Naturally, your house is going to take up much of the pa-kua when it is laid over the whole property. This is why many people use the pa-kua over different areas of their garden, rather than place it over the entire property (Figure 2B).

The pa-kua works well with square and oblong lots. Unusually shaped pieces of land are missing parts of the pa-kua, and these problems need to be rectified. The lights mentioned in the previous chapter prove helpful in this regard. However, if a piece of land is missing, say, the Marriage area, special attention should be given to this area in other parts of the garden.

You may, for instance, also place the pa-kua over your back garden plan. You can activate the Marriage

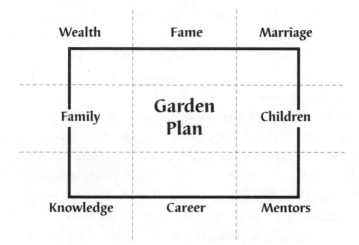

Wealth	Fame	Marriage
Family	**Garden Plan**	Children
Knowledge	Career	Mentors

**Figure 2B: Overlay your garden plan
with the pa-kua**

sector in this pa-kua to help make up for the lack of it
in the larger pa-kua placed over the whole property.

Wealth

The top left-hand corner of the pa-kua relates to wealth.
If the pa-kua was laid over a plan of your property, this is
the area located diagonally as far as it is possible to go to
the left from your main entrance.

If you want to increase your wealth, you need to activate this area in some way. You could plant flowers that
are the colors of your element or the one preceding it in
the productive cycle of the elements. Yellow and gold

flowers, such as dandelions, work well in the wealth sector since these colors symbolize money. You might have a pond or fountain here, as water symbolizes money in feng shui. Metal also relates to money, so a metal garden seat might be appropriate.

Certainly, this area would have to be well cared for. The condition of this part of your property will reflect the condition of your finances. Consequently, if it is full of weeds, or dead and dying plants, your fortunes are likely to suffer. Conversely, if this area is well tended, with attractive plants and shrubs, your fortunes will benefit. Naturally, anything that is dying should be removed immediately and replaced with something that is healthy, vigorous and attractive.

Spring daffodils work well in this location. Make sure that you plant more yellow ones than you do white. According to ancient tradition, this ensures that you will always have more gold than silver.

Fame

Next to the Wealth sector, in the middle of the back area of your lot, is the Fame area. Usually, this area relates to one's position and standing in the community. However, it can also refer literally to fame, if that is what you seek.

If you want to increase your reputation or become famous, you should activate this part of your garden in some way. Tall flowers and plants could symbolize your upward progress. You may want to place an outdoor seat here, so that you have a place to sit down comfort-ably and make plans.

Many people find comfort in talking to their plants. The Fame area is the perfect place to sit and tell your plants about your hopes and dreams. You can address your plants together or individually. Pierre Philion of the Department of Agriculture in Quebec cares for half a million apple trees and manages to talk to every single one of them.[1]

Marriage

The Marriage area is diagonally to the right as far as it is possible for you to go from your front entrance. Nowa-days, the Marriage area represents close relationships. If you are looking for such a relationship, or are wanting to improve an existing relationship, you should activate this area.

This is the perfect place to plant flowers that symbolize love and romance. Obviously, what you plant here depends on your particular location, but roses are usually a good choice. Roses were the first flowers to be domesti-cated, and have symbolized love and romance for thou-sands of years. A commercial rose grower told me that he always places a clove of garlic underneath any new rose he plants. The rose absorbs the garlic through the roots and this repels aphids.

If you have a seat in the Marriage sector, make sure that it can accommodate two people. If you are currently on your own, you need to make sure that both sides of the bench are used. If you always sit on the same side of the seat you are symbolically stressing the fact that you are single, rather than one half of a couple. By using both sides of the seat at different times, you will symbolically send the universe a message that you desire a partner. Obviously, you should ignore this if you want to remain on your own.

Family and Health

The Family and Health location is found diagonally to the left of the main entrance and consists of the middle third of the left-hand side of your property.

This area represents family in the wide sense of the term. It basically refers to people you are close to and care about. It also represents the health of the people living inside the house.

Naturally, this area should be well cared for, and flowers of as many colors as possible should be used. If someone in the household is unwell, plant flowers that relate to the color of the element preceding that person's personal element in the cycle of production.

If you are experiencing family problems, plant flowers of colors that relate to the personal elements of everyone in the household.

Good Luck Center

This area covers the entire center of the lot. In most cases, it is occupied by part of the house. Consequently, this area is usually activated only when the pa-kua is applied to a garden occupying a portion of the property.

This location is also known as the Spiritual Center. It is a good place to have a fountain or bird bath. Alternatively, a pergola, bower, aviary, large rock, or anything else that acts as a focal point for the garden will work well.

Plants that evoke feelings of spirituality should be used here as well. I find that purple flowers seem to do well in this location.

Children

The Children location is in the middle of the right-hand side of the lot. It relates to young people and their well-being. It also relates to the inner child inside all of us. This is a good place to let your imagination run wild. The more colorful this area is, the better. If you have young children, this is a good place to reserve a lawn for them to play on.

This area should be activated if you want children, or are having problems with your children. In the latter case, you should choose colors of the element that precedes their personal element in the cycle of production.

Knowledge

The Knowledge location is on the left-hand side of the lot, immediately in front of the Family location. It relates to knowledge, learning, and ultimate wisdom.

This is a good place to plant fruit trees and any other long-lived plants. Friends of mine have planted an oak tree in this area of their garden. They know they will not live long enough to see it grow to its full height, but to them it represents wisdom and serenity.

Career

The Career location comprises the middle third of the front of the property. This area should be enhanced to help you progress in your chosen career. As the entrance to the property is usually in the Career location, you should use bright, cheerful and appealing plants to encourage the ch'i onto the property, and ultimately into the house.

If you are not happy with the way your career is going, you can activate this area with flowers that relate to your personal element.

Mentors and Travel

The Mentors and Travel area is on the right-hand side of the main entrance to the property, alongside the Career area and in front of the Children location. There is an old saying that when the pupil is ready, the teacher will come. You can speed up this process by activating this area.

If you are wanting to travel, you may, depending on the climate, be able to plant shrubs, flowers, and trees that remind you of the places you want to visit.

The Aspirations of the pa-kua is intended to be a guide. There are no hard and fast rules. Naturally, you want to lay out your garden in a way that is intuitively satisfying to you. You may not be able to plant fruit trees in the Knowledge location because of the specific layout and geographical conditions of your garden. You may simply not want to have fruit trees in that location. Aesthetically, it might be totally wrong.

The best place to plant fruit trees, or anything else, for that matter, is where you think they will thrive and be happy. The Aspirations of the pa-kua can assist you in making informed decisions that will increase the level of ch'i on your property, and should be used as an enhancement in *partnership* with your aesthetic eye and the characteristics of your land, not in place of these things.

3

A New Garden

You are fortunate if you are able to start your garden from scratch. Most people buy a property and have to either live with or modify what already exists there.

Many buyers of new homes, particularly in large subdivisions, have no garden whatsoever. This provides them with a wonderful opportunity to create a garden that both enhances their property and creates as much ch'i as possible.

Be careful if you are buying in a new development. Check that all of the lots are approximately the same size. You will want all the houses in the completed project to be approximately equal in size and value, since a house that is out of proportion to the others will affect the ch'i of the entire neighborhood. If possible, buy a lot that is rectangular in shape. Shapes that are triangular, L or T-shaped create particular feng shui problems. Although these can be resolved, it is better to avoid them in the first place, if at all possible.

Do not buy a lot that is at the far end of a dead end street (Figure 3A). This is because the other residents will use up all the ch'i before it reaches your home. Do not buy a lot that has a road heading directly toward it—this creates a potentially dangerous shar.

Check the surrounding vegetation to see if it looks rich and lush. Frequently, developers remove all the

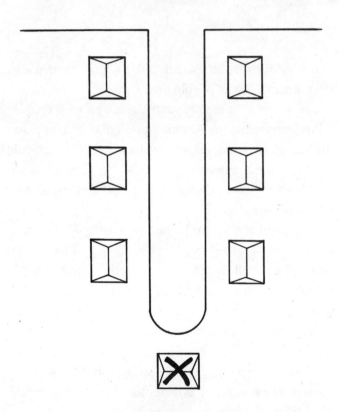

Figure 3A: Do not buy the house at the far end of a dead end street

existing vegetation to make their task easier. Until new growth has occurred, very little ch'i will be produced. However, in well-designed developments, the ch'i may actually be greater once the project has been completed than it was before.

Visit the lot you intend to buy at different times of the day and in different weather conditions. You may find that the site suffers from strong winds that carry all the beneficial ch'i away. You may discover something that blocks the sun from your property for part of each day. You may find that water settles on your site and takes a long time to drain away. It is better to become aware of these potential problems *before* you buy the lot, rather than afterward.

Naturally, the way you choose to lay out your garden will not be the same as my way. The ultimate arrangement depends on what your plan is for using the garden. The old adage "there is nothing new under the sun" is true to a large extent in garden design.

There are a number of established garden styles that are instantly recognizable. It is often a good idea to base your initial design on one of the standard styles, and then make whatever personal changes you desire to it. This will give you a foundation to work from, and will establish continuity throughout the garden.

Obviously, whatever style you choose will have to harmonize with your house. A highly formal, stylized garden might be perfect for a large Georgian manor house, but would look ridiculous around a small cottage that is falling to pieces. In fact, the type of home you have is likely to play a major part in whatever style you decide to use. Some of the most common styles include formal, cottage, Mediterranean, zen, courtyard, herb, mixed, and secret gardens.

Formal

In the past, a formal garden was completely symmetrical, each side being a mirror image of the other. Nowadays, that is not so important. Today, a formal garden is still laid out in a regular, geometrical pattern, but perfect symmetry is not required. You are likely to find stylized plants, well-trimmed hedges and lawns, paths leading to gazebos, avenues of trees, beautifully framed views, and formal pools and ponds. The formal garden relies on contrast and balance. Most gardeners find it hard to stay within this formal framework and tend to soften the effect with plants that traditionally would not be used.

Cottage

The cottage style is related to the formal style, as a degree of formality is still present. However, whereas a formal garden is kept severely in check, a cottage gardener allows the plants to spread and grow, eliminating harsh edges and creating a feeling of casualness.

In the past, the cottage style included a mixture of almost everything—except for shrubs. Today, simplicity is the keynote. Often herbs and vegetables are planted alongside hardy perennials. Scented flowers and fruit trees are popular.

Nostalgia plays a role in the popularity of the cottage garden. For instance, it is important to create an old-fashioned feel by using materials that are, or at least look, authentic. Furthermore, the naturalness of the cottage garden is soothing to the soul, and time spent inside a garden like this can help relieve the stress and strain of our hectic lifestyles.

Mediterranean

The Mediterranean style is popular all around the world, particularly in locations where the summer is hot and dry, and winters are mild. A Mediterranean garden allows for a balance of sun and shade. There is always plenty of room for outside living. Courtyards that can be used for both formal dining and relaxation are popular. Tiles, terra-cotta pots and white surfaces are all part of this style.

Naturally, the plants must be able to thrive in extremely dry conditions. Evergreen plants are essential in this garden, as they provide color in winter and shade in the summer. A multitude of bright colors can be used—the intense sunlight tends to soften them. Feng shui means "wind and water," and not surprisingly, irrigation is an essential requirement of the Mediterranean garden.

Zen

The Japanese zen garden is a masterpiece of simplicity (Figure 3B). In Japan, they are considered to be places of serenity, spirituality and contentment. It is rare to find a true zen garden in the West, but we can absorb the ideas of serenity, spirituality and contentment for use in our own gardens. The careful use of space is designed to draw you in to the garden while simultaneously keeping you at a distance.

Figure 3B: Japanese garden

A zen garden is usually a combination of gravel (or sand) and rock. The rocks form islands in a sea of gravel, and the gravel is carefully raked to create the effect of waves breaking on the islands.

Plants play a role, but they are carefully controlled and never allowed to run wild. Water is important also, with small appealing lakes and ponds adding coolness and interest to the scene. Trickling streams and small waterfalls create a background sound that is both peaceful and restoring to the soul.

Water and plants are carefully positioned to represent the path of nature. For instance, in the famous rock garden at the Ryoan-ju temple in Kyoto, the fine white gravel represents the oceans, while the rocks depict small islands in the sea. The clusters of rocks create sacred space for the gods.

Courtyard

Courtyard gardens probably date from Roman times. They reached their peak of popularity in the medieval monastery gardens (Figure 3C). The essential requirement is that the garden is at least partially surrounded by walls, usually from either the house itself or a neighboring property.

Courtyard gardens usually provide a great deal of privacy, making them ideal for outdoor entertaining. Traditionally, they were square or oblong, but nowadays any shape is acceptable. Friends of mine in Bath, England, have a triangular courtyard garden. They have filled up an otherwise dead space with a delightful entertaining area and garden.

Figure 3C: Courtyard garden

Herb

Herb gardens usually occupy part of a larger garden, though I have seen several gardens that were dedicated entirely to herbs. The ancient Romans planted herbs, along with vines, fruit, and vegetables, everywhere they went. This legacy was adopted by the monks in medieval times, and many of the herb gardens they planted are still thriving today.

Herb gardens are not only decorative, they are highly practical, offering a wide range of edible and medicinal herbs to choose from (see chapter 8).

Mixed

Most gardens fall into this category. They are character-ized by their mixture of flowering plants, fruit trees, veg-etables, and anything else that appeals to the gardener. I know someone who plants carrots on both sides of the winding path leading to his front door. In many gardens this would look totally out of place, but it works well with his personal mixed garden.

Most mixed gardens start without a plan, and gradu-ally change over the years as different owners put their preferences into play. Mixed gardens can be extremely attractive, and generally reveal more of their owners' per-sonalities than other type of garden. However, they sometimes create a confusing and muddled effect, which can be off-putting rather than attractive.

Secret

Everyone loves a secret. Can you remember the excite-ment you felt as a small child when someone told you a secret? A secret garden is a place where you can be entirely on your own to relax, meditate, and unwind. It is frequently an enclosed garden, protected from wind and erosion. The secret garden is so important in terms of feng shui that chapter 7 is devoted entirely to it. For further discussion and directions on how to make your own secret garden, please refer to that chapter.

Evaluating Your Property

You might want a formal garden that is beautifully laid out and manicured. You might have young children and want a garden that they can enjoy playing in. You might want to create a zen garden to help develop your spirituality. The number of ways that your garden can be laid out is unlimited. No matter how you decide to design it, the principles of feng shui can help you make the most of your garden and bring the maximum amount of ch'i into your home.

The first thing to look for is whether or not the property is protected at the back. The ancient Chinese believed that under every hill or mountain lived a green dragon or a white tiger. Where these two animals symbolically coupled was the perfect place to build a house. The dragon is always on the east side and the tiger on the west. Together they create a horseshoe-like arrangement that protects any house nestled within it.

Nowadays, it is rare to find a site that provides these qualities, and most people have to use neighboring houses to symbolically act as their dragons and tigers. Look at the land behind your house and see if it is protected by other houses, raised land, or trees. If it is not, you should plant some trees in your back yard to provide protection. Make sure that some of this planting extends to the sides of the house, gently surrounding the back in a protective semi-circle.

In the New Territories of Hong Kong, there are feng shui woods. These are crescent-shaped groves of trees that provide protection for a complete village. They contain the oldest trees in Hong Kong and, traditionally, only native plants were used. Nowadays, they usually plant trees that can benefit the whole village. Examples are the Joss Stick Tree, which is used for making incense, and fruits such as litchee and guava.[1] It would be unusual today for a group of neighbors to get together and provide protection for all their homes in this way. Most people have to provide their own symbolic protection.

Once the sides and back of your home are protected, you can look at the driveway and the path to your front door. These are the main routes the ch'i will take to get to your home. Winding or curved paths to your door are better than straight ones. They are more interesting and attractive, and help the smooth flow of ch'i. It is a good sign if your path widens slightly as it approaches the front door. The ch'i is constricted if it narrows at this point. The path and driveway should be well cared for. Dirt and weeds will create negative ch'i.

It is better for your land to be slightly elevated above the street. This means that when you approach your home you are heading upward, which is an auspicious sign and a portent of good fortune. It also means that when you leave the house you are heading downward. This is considered an "easy" direction, making forward progress that much easier to achieve.

Any steps should be wide and gradual. Narrow and steep steps have the potential to create bad luck and should be avoided.

You may want to have plants or trees on each side of the front entrance to act symbolically as guardians.

Friends of mine who have conifer trees gracing each side of their entrance refer to them as "soldiers"; they feel that the trees guard and protect the entire property.

You must ensure that nothing is planted directly in front of the front door of your house as this will block and restrict the ch'i. Likewise, trees that appear to lean toward the house will put subliminal pressure on the occupants. Trees that do this should be pruned or replaced to eliminate the constant, subtle stress and tension they create.

Flower beds on each side of the path leading to the front door provide color, fragrance, and excellent ch'i. Pots of brightly colored flowers beside the front door increase these benefits and make any visitors feel welcome (Figure 3D).

Check to make sure that none of the neighboring houses send shars toward your home. These could be caused by the corner of a house pointing toward you, or more frequently, by the roof line. If there are any shars like this, you will have to remedy them by symbolically making them disappear.

There are several methods for making a shar disappear: planting trees or hedges, erecting walls so that you can no longer see them, or, if this is not possible, you may have to put up a pa-kua mirror to symbolically reflect the shar back to where it came from.

Now it is time to look at the landscape of your property. Ideally, it should be flat or on a slight incline. Areas that are sunken denote potential problems. Placing a pa-kua over a plan of the lot will indicate the areas where these problems will arise. Lights placed in these sunken areas act as a remedy.

Look at the house itself. If it is not square or oblong in shape, you can symbolically finish the house off with

**Figure 3D: Pots of flowers beside the front door
are beneficial and provide ch'i**

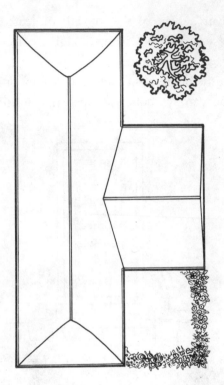

Figure 3E: Landscaping can symbolically finish off a house that is not square or oblong

careful landscaping (Figure 3E). Be careful when using fast-growing plants. They often create more problems than they cure, particularly if they get too tall. Remember that ch'i also enters the house through the windows. Consequently, you do not want to block off any windows with too many plants.

In fact, it is a good idea to go inside and look out each of the windows in turn, envisaging what you want to see.

Ideally, you want to create a beautiful scene from every window. Some judicious planting may be required to hide anything that creates a shar or appears ugly. People living a mile from us have planted a large hedge to conceal an ugly power transmitter from view.

Think about using water somehow in your front yard. Water is highly positive when it is in front of the house, and stimulates the flow of money toward you. A bird bath or small pond can make an attractive feature that also attracts money. However, you need to ensure that the source of water is *not* on your right-hand side when you look out the front door. There is an old feng shui belief that when a pond or fountain is situated on the right-hand side, money will come in but the husband is likely to stray.[2] Also note that water must be clean. Dirty water creates negative, or shar, ch'i.

A swimming pool is an expensive addition, but can help your finances if positioned correctly. Kidney-shaped pools should appear to embrace the house. This configuration assures your financial success. Water should appear to flow toward the house. Consequently, if your pool contains a fountain, this should be situated at the end farthest from the house to symbolically send the water toward you.

The sound of running water is a pleasing one that creates peace and harmony. Other sounds can be created by wind chimes, plants such as bamboo that rustle in the wind, and songbirds. All of these things make your garden a more pleasant place to be. In addition to ensuring pleasure, they also help attract and create ch'i.

If your lot is open to the road, you might want to erect a wall or hedge to provide some privacy. Walls and hedges can also reduce the traffic noise from busy roads, and eliminate any shars from a T-junction or from houses across the road. It is also a good idea to have a clear division between your property and the road.

The front garden is usually more formal than the back. Think about the overall effect you want to create. Do you want your property to attract favorable comments from passers by? Do you want to look successful? Do you want a property that almost looks after itself, or do you want a property you can work on all the time?

How your garden *looks* is important, of course, but try to incorporate color, scent, and sound in your garden as well. Personal preference comes into this. Over time, you will achieve a constantly changing, harmonious, and endlessly satisfying garden that characterizes you.

It is a good idea to use some of the same materials in the garden that were used on the house. Friends of ours live in a brick house, and have created brick borders for the flower beds in their front yard. This creates a feeling of continuity.

Use both yin and yang in the garden. This can be done in many ways. You can make effective use of light and shade, for instance. If your front garden receives sun all day long, you may want to plant some shade trees to provide balance and something to sit under. If your front garden is shaded, you might want to plant white flowers to create some yang in the yin environment.

The back garden is usually more private and casual. This is a good place to have a vegetable garden, fruit trees, a secret garden, a pleasant spot to sit outside and relax, or even a small wild space where plants can do whatever they wish.

You are fortunate if you are able to start laying out your back garden from scratch. If possible, you should arrange to have a small, secret, quiet spot where you can relax and be at peace with nature, protected from all the problems of the everyday world. We will discuss the secret garden in chapter 7.

When we bought our first home, an elderly neighbor came over and introduced himself. He told us sternly that we should have both a vegetable garden and a flower garden.

"Vegetables feed your stomach," he told us. "And flowers feed your soul."

He was right, of course. Many people overlook the vegetable garden, and consequently miss out on the pleasures of eating delicious fresh vegetables that are uncontaminated by chemical fertilizers and herbicides.

A vegetable garden can be placed anywhere, though it is usually located in the back garden, within easy reach of the kitchen. Many couples divide the garden up between them, with one partner looking after the vegetables while the other tends to the flowers. There is nothing wrong with this.

Any method that works is good. However, you might try placing your vegetable garden in the Marriage or

Family sectors and see what happens. One of the happiest couples I know has been married for more than sixty years. Tom and Sylvia credit the success of their marriage to the fact that they have always gardened together. Consequently, they have shared their triumphs and disasters. Tom's recipe for successful gardening is worth repeating. It could hardly be simpler:

"Grow plants that you love."

When you design a new garden you should also think about the wildlife in the neighborhood. All living things increase the feng shui of your garden. You can attract birds with a bird bath and hanging feeders. Naturally, these should be placed where you can enjoy them, while at the same time being out of reach of any cats. Birds are also attracted to berries.

You can attract other wildlife with native plants and a pond. Bees and butterflies are attracted by flowers. Hedges or walls made of rocks or logs attract a wide range of insects and small animals, like centipedes and hedgehogs.

Take your time. There is no need to do everything at once. Tackle a small part of your garden at a time. Ask for advice when you need it. Other gardeners are usually happy to offer advice and suggestions. Over the years I have found the staff in garden supply stores extremely helpful and knowledgeable. There are also many books available on gardening, as well as a number of videos and television programs.

4

Improving an Existing Garden with Feng Shui

Most people do not have the luxury of designing their own gardens. They have to make gradual adjustments to what is already there when they move to a new home. Look at your garden as dispassionately as possible—this may be difficult, especially if you have already put some time into gardening. You will see it from the point of view of what you have already achieved. If necessary, ask someone else to walk around your garden with you to point out items that do not feel right to them.

Some things might be glaringly obvious, while others are more subtle. When we moved into our current home, we immediately noticed an old, lichen-covered apple tree in the wealth area that was dying. In its day, it was probably productive and an enhancement to the wealth of the occupants, but now it was more likely to create negative ch'i than positive, so we removed it. As I believe in replacing any trees that have to be removed, we immediately planted two pear trees close to where the apple tree had been.

Is your lot rectangular in shape? Triangular, L and T-shaped lots create problems, though there are remedies to correct them. Outdoor lights and trees are the most usual remedies for lots that are irregular in shape. Ask yourself the following questions from the perspective of the road:

1. Does the garden appear to welcome you into the property?

2. Does it reflect your personality? Are there hills, neighbors or trees that symbolically provide protection to the back of your property?

3. Is the drive a gentle curve that gradually leads you to the front door?

4. Are there flower beds on each side of the path to create and attract ch'i energy?

5. Does anything cast shade on your property for any part of the day? A neighboring building, for instance, not only looks threatening if it is disproportionately large, but can also cast a shar of shade over the property for a period of time during the day.

Now look at the house itself, asking the following questions:

1. Is the house either too large or too small for the size of the property? In feng shui, we prefer the house to be approximately centered on the lot.

It does not matter if the back garden is slightly larger than the front, as this enables us to plant shrubs and trees behind the house as symbolic protection.

2. Is the garden in keeping with the style of the house? Are neighboring houses sending shars toward your home?

3. Are there any shars coming from your garden that affect your house?

4. Is the garage like an open mouth, ready to devour anyone who comes near?

The presence of a garage is a recent phenomenon in feng shui. It is considered a negative area full of stagnant ch'i energy. Rooms that are built on top of a garage are also negative, as it is believed that the vibrations of cars affect the energy flow and unsettle the occupants living above.

The ideal garage from a feng shui point of view is completely detached from the house itself. In this situation, the energy flow of the house is not affected by cars coming and going.

The worst position for a garage occurs when an important room, such as a bedroom, is immediately behind the garage (Figure 4A). This means that cars driving in are actually driving directly toward the person using this room. The remedy for this is to hang a mirror on both sides of the intervening wall. The mirror on the garage side must be placed with care so that the person

Figure 4A: The worst position for a garage

driving the car is not blinded by the glare of his or her own headlights.

The best driveways are circular or semi-circular, as these are believed to attract the ch'i and create good fortune. Nothing in nature creates a perfectly straight line. This is fortunate, as the ancient Chinese believed that ghosts traveled only along straight lines. Fortunately, a driveway that is perfectly straight can be softened by planting flower beds on each side.

It always seems strange to me that no one would dream of building a house without a plan, but few people draw even a simple sketch to provide some idea of what they want from their garden. Without a plan, you can waste a great deal of time, effort, and money on a garden that will be hard to look after and provide little or no pleasure.

The plan does not have to be elaborate; in fact, the simpler it is, the better. You have to decide what you want from your garden, take into account what is already there, and design accordingly. You will also have to consider how much time you have available to work in your garden. The amount of money at your disposal will determine what you can do now and what will have to wait until later.

Obviously, there will be structural elements that you can or will not want to change. A greenhouse, rock garden, concrete paths and swimming pool are all good examples. There will also be aspects of your lot that you *cannot* easily change. A steeply sloping piece of land could be leveled, but it would be an expensive and time-consuming task. You may have a beautiful tree that is in the wrong position. Although it might look better in another part of the garden, it is probably impractical to move it.

However, there are also many things that you *can* change, if you wish. A garden shed and the clothesline, for instance, could be moved without too much difficulty if you wanted them somewhere else.

Once you have drawn up a simple plan of your property, place a three-by-three magic square over it, aligning the bottom row (Knowledge, Career and Mentors) of this with the entrance to your property. This allows you to look at your property from the point of view of the different areas of life shown by the nine sections of the magic square. You may find that your Marriage area is a mass of weeds, and the Career area is where you store your trash until it is collected.

Examine each of the nine areas in turn, paying special attention to the areas that you want to improve. For instance, if you are seeking a partner or are having problems with your relationship, you will want to examine the Marriage area of your garden closely. Are there any plants or colors that remind you of love and romance in this part of your garden? Is this area cluttered up with weeds and non-romantic items such as a clothesline?

Write down any ideas you have for improving the areas of concern. Do not take any action at this stage. You will want to place the magic square over different parts of your property. For instance, you may want to lay it over the entire back garden, or perhaps a flower garden in the center of the front lawn.

In the next chapter, we will be learning how to use the compass directions to gain even more insight. Consequently, all of this needs to be taken into account before we make any changes.

Now that you have arranged the magic square over your property, possibly in a variety of ways, and analyzed the results, you will have many ideas about what you want to do with your garden.

With your results in mind, go out to the road and look at your property from the street. Walk up to the front door, using the route that your guests would take. Then go around the side of the house and look at the rest of the property. Try to do this as dispassionately as possible, so that you will see everything that a visitor would notice. Do the various parts of your garden create a pleasing whole? Are there areas that do not seem to harmonize with the rest of garden? Are there any major

problems, such as overhead power lines or a huge neighboring building that blocks out your sun?

Make notes about any problems that you see. Again,
make no major changes at this stage. It is a good idea,
though, to repair any minor problems that you see. For
instance, a dripping faucet should be fixed as soon as
you notice it. Water relates to money in feng shui, and a
dripping tap means that money is draining away.

This stage is a good time to visit your local garden
supply store. Ask questions about the plants you intend
to buy. You don't want to accidentally plant a shrub that
needs sun all day in a shady spot. You also need to know
how large the plant will become, how much water it will
need, and whether or not it sheds its leaves in the fall.

Once you have done all this, it is time to look at your
property again, using the compass directions. We will
learn how to do this in the next chapter.

5

Directions in the Garden

We have already placed the magic square over our garden by aligning it with the main entrance to the property. Now we are going to take it a step further by aligning the magic square using the compass directions.

Originally, the magic square was an octagonal shape called the pa-kua. Each of the eight sides indicated a compass direction, and each direction was connected to one of the trigrams of the I Ching.

The Chinese invented the compass some 2,200 years ago. Until then, feng shui had been mainly concerned with the geography of the landscape. Now, using a compass and a person's date of birth, it was possible to personalize feng shui for the occupants of any site. The original system of feng shui is known as the Form School. Not surprisingly, the system that uses the compass is known as the Compass School.

Nowadays, most feng shui practitioners use a combination of both schools in making their assessments. One

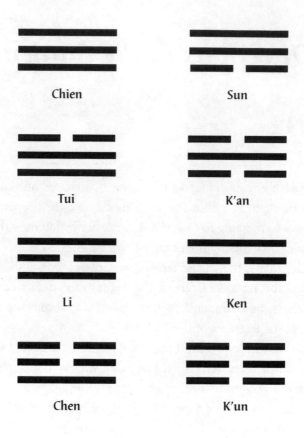

Figure 5A: The eight trigrams

hundred years ago that would have been unusual; until then, practitioners specialized in one school rather than utilizing both.

The Compass School

The magic square that Wu of Hsia discovered on the shell of a tortoise indicates the eight different compass directions as well as the center. Each compass direction was given one of the eight trigrams from the I Ching (Figure 5A). The trigrams are every possible combination of straight and broken lines that can be placed into three lines. The straight lines represent yang energy and the broken lines depict yin energy.

These trigrams are placed into position in the magic square in an order known as the Latter Heaven Sequence. There are two important arrangements of the trigrams. The Former Heaven Sequence was devised by Wu of Hsia, and depicts a perfect universe. The Latter Heaven Sequence, devised by the Duke of Wen some 3,000 years ago, is a more practical arrangement that relates better to the world in which we live. Consequently, it is this sequence that is normally used.

The eight trigrams are placed into the following positions: Li goes in the south, K'an in the north, Chen in the east, and Tui in the west. Sun goes in the southeast, K'un in the southwest, Chien in the northwest, and Ken in the northeast (see Figure 5B).

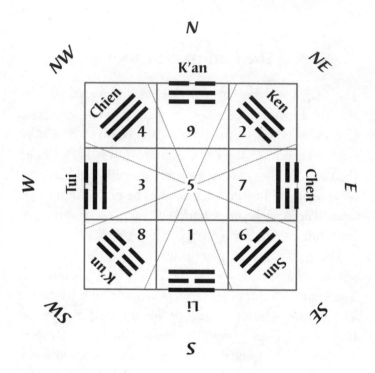

Figure 5B: Wu of Hsia's magic square overlaid by the compass positions of the eight trigrams

The Latter Heaven Sequence depicts the cycle of an entire year:

Chen (The Arousing) is in the east and represents spring, with its new beginnings and fresh promise.

Sun (The Gentle), in the southeast, depicts the time when small animals grow.

Li (The Clinging) is in the south and represents summer. It also shows that new life is not yet ready to leave the home or nest.

K'un (The Receptive) is in the southwest and represents good nourishment and the life that comes from the earth.

Tui (The Joyful) is in the west and symbolizes the start of fall. It is a happy time, but there is an awareness that winter is getting closer.

Chien (The Creative) is in the northwest and depicts late autumn. It symbolizes the endurance that will shortly be required, as winter is not very far away.

K'an (The Abysmal) is in the north. It represents winter, and the hard work that is necessary in order to survive.

Finally, **Ken** (Keeping Still), in the northeast, represents late winter and the ending of one cycle before the next one starts the whole process once more.

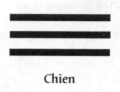

Chien

Chien—the Creative

Symbol:	Heaven
Keyword:	Strength
Element:	Sky
Season:	Late Fall
Direction:	Northwest
Color:	Mauve

Chien is made up of three unbroken lines, and consequently depicts pure yang energy. It is related to energy, determination and perseverance. Chien relates to the head of the family, usually the father. It is also associated with stamina and strength.

This area of the garden should be activated when anyone in the household is starting anything new.

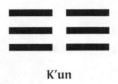

K'un

K'un—the Receptive

Symbol: Earth
Keyword: Obedience
Element: Earth
Season: Late Summer
Direction: Southwest
Color: Pink

K'un is made up of three broken (yin) lines, and depicts pure yin energy. It represents close relationships, especially that of a husband and wife, though it can also represent father and son or even master and servant. K'un relates particularly to the mother.

This area of the garden can be activated to encourage cooperation, peace and contentment.

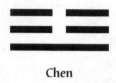

Chen

Chen—the Arousing

Symbol:	Thunder
Keyword:	Progress
Element:	Wood
Season:	Early Spring
Direction:	East
Color:	Green

Chen is made up of two broken (yin) lines above an unbroken (yang) line. It represents the eldest son. Chen relates to decisiveness and unexpected occurrences.

This area of the garden can be activated to enhance wisdom and learning.

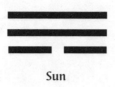

Sun

Sun—the Gentle

Symbol:	Wind
Keyword:	Penetration
Element:	Wood
Season:	Late Spring
Direction:	Southeast
Color:	Purple

Sun consists of one broken (yin) line beneath two unbroken (yang) lines. It represents the eldest daughter. Sun relates to innate goodness, a good mind and inner strength. It can also represent purity and wholeness.

This area can be activated to attract prosperity into the household.

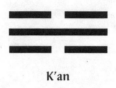

K'an

K'an—the Abysmal

Symbol:	Water
Keyword:	Entrapment
Element:	Water
Season:	Early Winter
Direction:	North
Color:	Black

K'an is made up of one unbroken (yang) line between two broken (yin) lines. It represents the middle son. K'an relates to drive, ambition and hard work.

This part of the garden should be activated to encourage happy and loving relationships.

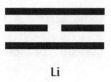

Li

Li—the Clinging

Symbol:	Fire
Keyword:	Magnificence
Element:	Fire
Season:	Early Summer
Direction:	South
Color:	Red

Li is composed of a broken (yin) line between two unbroken (yang) lines. It relates to the middle daughter. Li represents beauty, laughter, warmth and dryness. It is also associated with brilliance and success.

This part of the garden can be activated to increase the reputation and standing of the inhabitants.

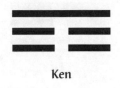

Ken

Ken—Keeping Still

Symbol:	Mountain
Keyword:	Pause
Element:	Earth
Season:	Late Winter
Direction:	Northeast
Color:	Blue

Ken is composed of two broken (yin) lines beneath an unbroken (yang) line. It relates to the youngest son. Ken represents solitude, stability, consolidation and patient waiting.

This area of the garden should be activated to enhance loving times with children and other family members.

Tui

Tui—the Joyful

Symbol: Mouth
Keyword: Joy
Element: Lake
Season: Early Fall
Direction: West
Color: White

Tui is made up of two unbroken (yang) lines beneath a broken (yin) line. It relates to the youngest daughter. Tui represents happiness, pleasure and satisfaction.

This part of the garden can be activated to create pleasure and encourage a sense of fun and play.

Your Property's Trigram

To determine your property's individual trigram, stand at your main street frontage with a compass and see what direction you are facing. Strangely enough, this is not the most important direction. The direction the *back* of your property faces determines which trigram relates to your piece of land. This direction is called where the back "sits." Consequently:

Li property sits to the south and faces north.

K'un property sits to the southwest and faces northeast.

Tui property sits to the west and faces east.

Chien property sits to the northwest and faces southeast.

K'an property sits to the north and faces south.

Ken property sits to the northeast and faces southwest.

Chen property sits to the east and faces west.

Sun property sits to the southeast and faces northwest.

You can activate the essence of the different trigrams by having plants of the appropriate color in the different sections. Naturally, you would not exclude every color except red in the Li area. However, by accenting this color, along with a variety of other colors, you can reap the feng shui benefits.

You can use the trigrams along with the Aspirations of the pa-kua (page 20) to plan a successful garden. Simply place an overlay of the Aspirations of the pa-kua over a plan of your property as we did in chapter 2. But now, include an overlay of the eight trigrams with Ken, K'an and Chien aligned with your street frontage (Figure 5C). Just as before, you can also overlay your garden plan.

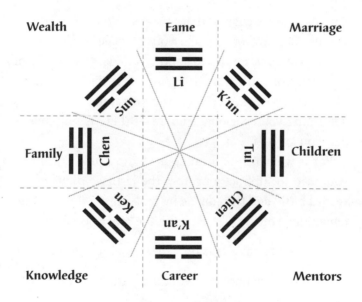

Street Frontage

**Figure 5C: Aspirations of the pa-kua and
the eight trigrams properly aligned
to the front of your property**

Remember the principles of yin and yang to create balance and harmony. You might decide to have some yin (or cool-colored) flowers in a yang (sunny) part of your garden or property. Likewise, some yang (or hot-colored) flowers will help raise the ch'i in a yin (cool) part of your garden.

Your Personal Trigram

You also have a trigram that relates to you. The formula you use depends on whether you are male or female.

For a man, you need to subtract the last two digits of your year of birth from 100, and then divide by nine. The answer is ignored, but the remainder is used to determine your personal trigram. If there is no remainder, you are a Li.

For a woman, the formula is slightly different. First, you need to subtract four from the last two digits of the year of birth, and then divide by nine. Again, if there is no remainder, you are a Li. Here are the other possibilities:

If the remainder is one, the person is a **K'an**.

If the remainder is two, the person is a **K'un**.

If the remainder is three, the person is a **Chen**.

If the remainder is four, the person is a **Sun**.

If the remainder is five, the person is a **K'un** if male, or a **Ken** if female.

If the remainder is six, the person is a **Chien**.

If the remainder is seven, the person is a **Tui**.

If the remainder is eight, the person is a **Ken**.

And, of course, if there is no remainder, the person is a **Li**.

The East and West Four Houses

The eight trigrams can be divided into two groups. The East Four Houses include Li, K'an, Chen and Sun. The West Four Houses consist of Chien, K'un, Ken and Tui.

You are likely to be happiest living on a property that belongs to the same trigram as you. However, you would also feel content living on a property that belongs to the same group as you. Consequently, if you are a Li and your property is Chen, you would immediately feel perfectly at home. This would not be the case if you were a Li living on a Ken property, as these trigrams belong to different groups.

Obviously, some compromises may have to be made, since frequently a number of people live on the same property. In the past, the trigram of the man of the house was always the one that was important. Nowadays, it is usually the trigram of the person who brings the most money into the home that is considered. In the garden, though, it is the trigram of the person who does most of the maintenance for the garden that should be used. The house and the individual rooms inside it can all be arranged according to the person who uses them most.

Positive and Negative Directions

In feng shui there are four positive and four negative directions. They are more important inside the house than they are in the garden, but still need to be considered when examining the garden as a whole.

Every property is divided into eight sections determined by the compass: north, northeast, east, southeast, south, southwest, west, and northwest. For every property, four of these are positive in nature. In feng shui, the positive directions are *prime, health, longevity,* and *prosperity.* The other four are negative directions. In feng shui they are *death, disaster, six shar,* and *five ghosts.* In a Chen house, east, north, southeast and east are considered positive directions, while west, southwest, northeast and northwest are considered negative. Figure 5D (page 76) shows the positive and negative directions for every house.

The Positive Directions

Prime. The Prime direction is always at the back of the garden, as it is always the direction that the garden sits toward. This area is also known as *Fu Wei,* which means "good life." Consequently, this part of the garden is an excellent area to use as a place to relax and unwind, away from the stress and pressure of everyday life. It is also a good location for a bird bath, small pond, or fountain.

Health. This direction brings vitality, good health and genuine friends. Brightly colored flowers in this part of the garden are beneficial for anyone in the family who is not feeling well. It is best to have flowers that relate to the element that precedes the sick person's element. This is because they help create the following element, thus providing energy and strength for the ill person.

Longevity. This direction attracts peace, harmony, good health and feelings of youthfulness. Activating this area will help ease family disagreements and other problems.

Prosperity. This is the most auspicious direction of all. In China it is called *Sheng Ch'i*, which means "generating good ch'i." When activated, this direction can attract upward progress, financial success, vitality, and peace of mind. Asians enjoy gambling and like to face this direction when playing games of chance, in the belief that it will increase their luck.

The Negative Directions

The negative directions are of more importance inside the house than they are in the garden. However, I am including them for the sake of completeness.

The negative directions indicate good areas for compost bins, clotheslines, and trash storage. They are not good directions for outdoor entertaining, or for doing anything that contains an element of danger, such as chopping wood.

Property Sits Toward	Chien	K'un	Ken	Tui	Li	K'an	Chen	Sun
	NW	SW	NE	W	S	N	E	SE
Prime	NW	SW	NE	W	S	N	E	SE
Health	NE	W	NW	SW	SE	E	N	S
Longevity	SW	NW	W	NE	N	S	SE	E
Prosperity	W	NE	SW	NW	E	SE	S	N
Death	S	N	SE	E	NW	SW	W	NE
Disaster	SE	E	S	N	NE	W	SW	NW
Six Shar	N	S	E	SE	SW	NW	NE	W
Five Ghosts	E	SE	N	S	W	NE	NW	SW

Figure 5D: Positive and negative directions for each trigram

Death. The Death direction is traditionally considered the worst direction of all. It is related to accidents, illness, and other misfortunes. The Chinese word for this direction is *Chueh Ming*, which means "total catastrophe."

Disaster. This direction is related to anger, arguments, and legal problems. It is not a good idea to entertain your friends in this part of the garden!

Six Shar. This direction is related to procrastination, loss, and scandal.

Five Ghosts. This direction is related to fire, theft, and financial problems.

It is a good idea to face one of your four favorable directions when doing anything important or when you want to make a good impression. You may, for example, be entertaining some important people in your garden. In this situation, it would be advantageous to sit in a chair facing one of your favorable directions.

Fortunately, it is easy to determine your favorable directions. If your property belongs to the East Four Houses group, then north, south, east and southeast are your positive directions. If your property belongs to the West Four Houses, then west, southwest, northeast and northwest are your favorable directions.

You may want to have plants of the right colors to enhance each direction. Doing this will increase the effect of your positive directions, and ease the negative aspects of your other directions. We will look at colors and fragrances in greater depth in the next chapter.

6

Colors and Fragrances

I know a bank where the wild thyme blows,

Where oxlips and the nodding violet grows,

Quite over-canopied with luscious woodbine,

With sweet musk-roses and with eglantine:

There sleeps Titania sometime of the night,

Lull'd in these flowers with dances and delight...

—William Shakespeare,
A Midsummer Night's Dream

Color and smell are two of the most obvious ways that plants enhance our environments. Color and smell can also be used effectively in feng shui as remedies and enhancements.

The effects that different colors have on us is fascinating and is being studied more and more by behavioral psychologists.[1] For instance, red raises your blood pressure, while blue slows it down.[2] Caterers have long known that orange stimulates the appetite and encourages people to eat quickly. Warm colors promote feelings of excitement, while cooler colors create feelings of relaxation and peace. The colors we choose to wear affect how we are perceived by others.

Fragrances affect our emotions in the same way. Memories from the past are easily triggered by different smells.

We can enhance any part of our garden by planting flowers of the correct color for that location. The colors are determined by the compass directions that correspond to each part of the garden. In the last chapter, we discussed the basic colors for each direction. Here they are again, in greater detail:

> The **East** direction relates to the trigram Chen and the colors brown and green. This part of your garden relates to health.

> The **Southeast** direction relates to the trigram Sun and the colors red, green, blue and purple. This part of your garden relates to money and prosperity.

> The **South** direction relates to the trigram Li and the colors red and orange. This part of your garden relates to your personal power and standing in the community.

> The **Southwest** direction relates to K'un and the colors pink, red, and white. This part of your garden relates to love and marriage.

The **West** direction relates to Tui and the colors white and silver. This part of your garden relates to children, pets, and creativity.

The **Northwest** direction relates to the trigram Chien and the colors white, gray, black, and mauve. This part of your garden relates to travel, mentors, and other people who can help you.

The **North** direction relates to the trigram K'an and the colors clear (as in water), blue, and black. This part of your garden relates to your career.

The **Northeast** direction relates to the trigram Ken and the colors green, blue, and black. This part of your garden relates to knowledge and learning.

The **center** relates to the colors yellow and orange. This part of your garden relates to peace and spirituality.

These directions correspond to each individual garden that you have. For instance, you may use it over the plan of your entire property, or alternatively, use it separately over different flower beds or different areas of your garden. If you have a secret garden, you will want to use these directions to choose suitable colors for your quiet place.

Also, you can improve any area of your life by using the colors that relate to that subject. For instance, if you want to develop spiritually, you would benefit by planting daffodils (or any yellow or orange flower) in the center of your garden. Likewise, if you want more money, you should plant red, green, blue, or purple flowers in the southeast. In this instance, you might also want to activate the Career area (the north) of your garden.

The Five Flowers of Feng Shui

Traditionally, five flowers are considered to be the most important in feng shui. This is because of the blessings and benefits they provide to their owners. These five flowers are: peonies, chrysanthemums, white magnolias, orchids, and lotuses (Figure 6A).

Peony

The peony is a native of Mongolia and Siberia, and is the most important of the five flowers. It represents wealth and honor. It also symbolizes love. When it flowers, it represents great fortune. In China it is sometimes known as "the plant of twenty days," as its blossoms remain fresh for almost three weeks. The tree peony is reputed to live for more than 120 years.[3]

The peony can help your relationship if planted in the southwestern part of your garden. In China, the presence of peonies inside the house means that the family has unmarried, eligible daughters.

**Figure 6A: The five most important feng shui
flowers, clockwise from bottom: white magnolia,
chrysanthemum, orchid, lotus, and peony**

Chrysanthemum

The chrysanthemum is a native of China and represents
happiness and laughter. Chrysanthemums are frequently
found in Chinese homes, as they symbolize comfort, happiness, and a pleasant life. They are also related to nobil-
ity and strength of character.

White Magnolias and Orchids

White magnolias and orchids symbolize good taste and femininity. In China the white magnolia is considered to represent purity and truth. The Chinese also used the bark and the flower buds as herbal remedies.

Lotus

The Buddhists and Hindus both consider the lotus to be a sacred flower that symbolizes purity. The Buddhists consider the lotus to symbolize Buddha—he appeared floating on a huge lotus, with a smaller lotus in his hand. Vishnu, the Hindu god, also appeared floating on nine golden lotus plants. In the garden, the lotus represents peace, purity, tranquility, and spiritual growth. It can also enhance creativity.

Choosing Colors

Color choice is something that is personal to each of us. This makes it impossible to give advice on specific shades of color, and on which colors go better with other colors. I once visited a garden that contained a huge bed of red flowers of every conceivable shade. The initial effect was jarring, but I soon became used to it and found the combinations effective. However, the person I was with thought it was one of the ugliest gardens she had ever seen.

The owner of the garden was a psychiatrist who had created the red garden deliberately to see what effect it would have on people. He found that it gave everybody a shock when they first saw it, but after a few minutes, approximately half the viewers became used to it and many grew to love it, but the other half never got used to it. This particular bed was in the psychiatrist's relationship area, but I wasn't brave enough to ask him what effect all that red was having on his personal life.

Naturally, some colors match better than others, and we all try to create effective combinations in our gardens. However, the colors that I think go well together may be quite different from the colors that you think harmonize. It is important to realize that in the wild, the incredible profusion of color creates a homogenous whole. Consequently, it is a waste of time arguing about which colors are better matched—there is no correct answer.

Red

Red is the most dramatic color of all and creates a striking effect in the garden. In a garden of flowers, the red ones are usually noticed first. Red can boost your spirits and morale. If you are feeling tired and lethargic, a short time in the garden looking at your red flowers will increase your energy.

There is a huge array of red-colored flowers to choose from. Naturally, roses always top the list of popular red flowers, and there are certainly an abundance of them to choose from.

I've always loved the scalloped leaves and fire-red flowers of the pelargonium (*geranium*). My wife prefers the velvety feel of the five-petaled pansy, which is available in many colors in addition to red. Other favorites are the Red Hot Poker (*knifophia uvaria*), fuchsia, chrysanthemum, and the oriental poppy (*papaver orientale*) with its large, floppy, silky-textured red and black flower.

Obviously, the flowers you choose will depend on your location and climate. We live in a temperate climate at sea level. Naturally, the flowers we plant in our garden will not be the same as yours if you live at 5,000 feet and have a temperature ranging from zero degrees to more than a hundred.

Pink

Pink is the most feminine color and relates to the emotions. It is a gentle, nurturing color that offers care, protection and support. It is no wonder that pink is considered the color of love.

My mother loved begonias, and I am always reminded of my childhood whenever I see their beautiful pink and white flowers. Cyclamen also come in different shades of pink and white. Cinerarias come in a variety of colors, including a delicate pink. The Ball dahlia is a gorgeous round flower held singly on long, erect stems. They come in a wide range of colors, though pink is by far my favorite. Phlox, tulips, amaryllis, and peonies also represent peace and tranquility to me.

Orange

Orange is a warm, restless color that provides energy and positive feelings.

Sunflowers and ox-eye chamomile (*anthemis tinctoria*) are two of my favorite orange flowers. Sunflowers are large, while chamomile are small and daisy-like—but both have delightful powder-puff centers that I find highly appealing. Polyanthuses come in a wide range of colors, including a vibrant orange. Wallflowers are found in orange, yellow, and red. They can brighten up any garden. The Californian poppy can be almost bronze in color, but is more commonly found in orange, yellow, and ivory.

Yellow

In Imperial China, yellow was considered such a sacred color that only the emperor was allowed to wear it.[4] The Egyptians and Mayans related yellow to the sun and revered its power to sustain life. Yellow flowers can uplift and sustain you when your spirits are down. Yellow creates positive feelings, cheer and warmth wherever it is found. Incidentally, yellow flowers can also enhance your thought processes and communication skills.

One of the most unusual yellow flowers I have seen is the Lady's Slipper orchid (*cypripedium calceolus*), which has pouch-like flowers resembling a slipper or cradle. My late father-in-law grew orchids for many years, and it was the Lady's Slipper that piqued his interest in them in the first place.

Yellow onion grew wild in our neighborhood when I was growing up, and it always brings back happy memories. Daffodils are probably my favorite yellow flower, though it is hard to choose just one type from the huge array of daffodils available.

A young man I knew was promoted to the position of salesman for the corporation he worked for. He was a quiet, shy person and was concerned about his ability to communicate with the customers. I suggested that he plant daffodils in the Career area of his garden. These, accompanied by his determination, assured his success in the new position.

Green

Green is a caring, nurturing, healing color. It is in the center of the color spectrum and creates feelings of peace and harmony. Naturally, you will have plenty of green in your garden already, but there are a number of green flowers that you may want to plant as well.

Lady's Mantle (*alchemilia mollis*) creates a profusion of tiny creamy-green flowers. Bells of Ireland (*molucella laevis*) have spikes full of green bell-shaped flowers. Bear's Foot (*helleborus foetidus*) also has flowers in the shape of beautifully rounded green bells, with white stamens that resemble clappers. The common climbing ivy (*hedera helix*) makes a cheerful display. It has small, green flowers that cluster together in groups and attract bees.

Blue

Blue enhances creativity. It also relates to hope, trust and optimism. When you need an answer to a difficult problem or are feeling negative, you can benefit by spending time with the color blue.

The Sorcerer's violet (*vinca major*), with the square-topped petals of its mauve-blue flowers, is a good example of a beautiful blue flower. Blue pimpernel (*anagalis linifolia*), lobelia (*lobelia tenuior*) and the grape hyacinth (*muscari neglectum*) are also fine examples.

When I was a child my mother had a row of Agapanthus lilies (*agapanthus campanulatus*) in front of our house. The slightly faded blue of those flowers contrasted beautifully with their long and shiny leaves.

Two of my favorite plants have gorgeous sky-blue flowers. These are the blue delphinium and the Himalayan poppy (*meconopsis betonicifolia*).

Violet

Violet is the color of thought, spirituality, and tranquility. It also relates to intuition, thoughtfulness, and concern for others. Undoubtedly, the most famous violet-colored flower of all is the sweet violet itself.

In ancient Greece, the violet symbolized the might of Athens. In medieval times, the blooms were used as sweeteners before sugar became available. Violets were also used as a deodorant. In Victorian times, street hawkers offered violets to passers by.[5] It is strange that after World War I, the beautiful sweet violet suddenly became neglected.

There are many violet, mauve, purple, and lilac flowers to choose from. When I first stayed with friends in Wiltshire, England, I could not get over their front garden. It was full of Sea Holly (*eryngium oliverianum*). The puff-ball heads of these flowers are like pin cushions that seem to be resting on purple stars. Unfortunately, I have had little success in growing them myself.

Other good examples of purple flowers are heliotrope (*heliotropium peruvianum*), ivy-leaf pelargonium (*pelargonium peltatum*), Virginian cowslip (*mertensia virginica*), and some shades of petunia (which can also be found in almost every color imaginable).

White

White is usually considered the color of purity and innocence. It is also related to illumination, inspiration, spirituality, and love. I particularly like the peaceful and serene look of white flowers at dusk and early evening.

It is no surprise that white roses are so popular. There are many to choose from, but my favorite is probably the *floribunda* rose, frequently known as "Iceberg."

Have you ever experienced the sense of peace and tranquility brought on by coming across a garden full of snow-in-summer (*cerastium tomentosum*)? These are small, herbaceous plants with numerous flowers that seem to entirely cover the plant.

The white snowdrop (*gelanthus rivalis*) has flowers that look like tiny ballerinas dancing in the wind. The lily of the valley has beautiful flowers that look like small, perfectly round bells. The pelargonium has several flowers clustered together to make one large rounded bouquet of perfectly pure white. These are all personal favorites of mine, but there are thousands upon thousands of other white flowers to choose from.

Some gardeners use a color wheel to choose harmonizing and contrasting colors. I prefer to use my feelings about what looks right. It can be great fun choosing the right colors, and all that matters is that you are happy with the overall effect.

We also need to take into account the balance of bright and pastel colors. The bright colors (red, white, yellow and some blues) are exciting and have a tendency to dominate the garden—they can easily overpower the more subtle colors. Consequently, they need to be used with care.

In the end, it all comes down to personal preference. This is why gardens so clearly reveal the personalities of their owners. Try to create a harmonious balance in your garden, but do not be afraid to experiment with different colors.

Choosing Fragrances

One of the most enjoyable aspects of being in a garden is the variety of delicate fragrances that we are exposed to. I remember, as a teenager, taking an elderly blind lady to a botanical garden. She put me to shame by identifying the vast majority of plants from their perfumes alone.

Have you ever noticed how a fragrance can instantly bring back long-forgotten memories? Just recently, the smell of scented geraniums took me back to when I was at preschool. Scented geraniums provide fragrance only when the leaves come into contact with something else. I am ashamed to admit that I, along with the other children, eventually destroyed all the geraniums as we savored their fragrance.[6] Honeysuckle always reminds me of lazy summer vacations at the beach. Roses bring back a variety of memories—some happy, others not.

When I learned about Napoleon in high school, our teacher brought in a bunch of violets. The love story of Napoleon and Josephine returns to me in vivid detail whenever I smell the fragrance of violets. In the past, violets were loved because of their color, odor and even taste. Wine used to be made from them, and even today, it is possible to occasionally find violet marmalade and violet tea. The prophet Mohammed described the unforgettable smell of violets well when he said:

> . . . as my religion is above all others, so is the excellence of the odor of violets above all others. It is warmth in winter and coolness in summer.[7]

The pleasing scent comes from an essential oil that is produced inside the flowers of aromatic plants. In herbs, this essential oil is produced in the leaves. The chemical structure of the oil, known as an attar, is relatively simple in the case of herbs, but it is highly complex in other plants, with each species having its own highly complicated formula.

Fragrant plants can be placed anywhere, but the perfect spot is a sheltered one where the fragrance will not be wafted away. A gazebo, arbor, or wall can be enhanced enormously with the addition of a climbing plant that has a pleasing fragrance. Honeysuckle, clematis, and jasmine are good examples of fragrant climbing plants. There are many climbing roses to choose from as well.

There are even fragrant lawns that provide scent when walked on. A good example is the chamomile lawn, which is particularly fragrant after a shower of rain. Peppermint and spearmint also create wonderful aromatic lawns. Creeping zinnia provides an excellent groundcover and spreads rapidly. It provides a profusion of yellow flowers as well as a delightful scent. Fragrant lawns are guaranteed to bring squeals of delight from your friends. I could never forget how excited I was when I unexpectedly came across a thyme lawn at Sissinghurst castle in Kent, England, many years ago.

Sweet-smelling shrubs can be placed in outdoor seating areas or patios to add greater pleasure to the scene. Chamomile, thyme, and different mints can be useful here as well. Many plants are most fragrant in the evening, and you might enjoy having these at your front gate to greet you when you return home from work. My parents planted Queen of the Night outside their bedroom window and it is still my favorite smell from childhood. Evening primrose and border phlox are other good examples of flowers that are scented in the evening.

It is a good idea to plant fragrant shrubs that flower in the winter. This ensures that you will get pleasure from your garden all year round. There are varieties of honey-suckle, cimomanthus praecox, daphnes, and viburnum that bloom in the winter months. The Japonica (*mahonia japonica*) is an attractive year round addition to the garden and provides garlands of beautifully scented yellow flowers from late fall to early spring.

Thousands of years ago, early humans wanted to take the scent of the garden indoors. Archaeologists have found jars of perfume more than 4,000 years old in Ancient Egyptian tombs. This fact is even more remarkable when you consider how difficult it is to make flower perfumes, even today. Perfume-making was also known to the ancient Chinese, Hindus, Israelites, Carthaginians, Greeks, and Romans.[8]

Fortunately, we can easily take the fragrance indoors in other ways by using a variety of freshly cut flowers, potpourri, pomanders, and herb pillows.

Roses are probably renowned as much for their fragrance as for their color, beauty, and association with romance. Roses were loved by the ancient Persian, Greek, and Roman civilizations, and have inspired writers such as William Shakespeare ever since. Generally speaking, it is the antique roses that provide the greatest perfume. Entire valleys of the Kazanlik rose (*rosa trigintipetala*) were grown in Persia to produce attar of roses.[9] The most famous and fragrant of modern roses is the American Beauty, which sadly is not as readily available as it used to be. Professional gambler "Diamond Jim" Brady presented huge bouquets of this rose to the famous singer and actress Lillian Russell to express his devotion.[10]

Particularly fragrant roses include the Gallica, Damask, Musk, Bourbon, and Briar varieties, each with a large range of specimens to choose from.

There are countless other perfumed flowers to choose from. Heliotrope, honeysuckle, jasmine, jonquil, lilac, lily of the valley, pelargonium, peony, stock, and violet are all good examples, and have the advantage of being able to grow almost anywhere.

The Romans were the first to use perfumes to help induce sleep by adding dried rose petals to their pillows. Queen Elizabeth I had an entire mattress padded with Lady's Bedstraw (*galium odorata*). George III was unable to sleep without his hop pillow.[11] Victorian ladies used lavender cushions to avoid the "vapors." Mint pillows have long been believed to cure headaches. A friend of mine uses a pillow stuffed with pine needles whenever his nose is congested.

Lavender was introduced to Britain by the ancient Romans, who brought it with them to perfume their bath water. The name "lavender" comes from the Latin word *lavo*, which means "I wash." It is still just as popular today—probably because when it is dried, it retains its fragrance for longer than any other herb. Incidentally, lavender and roses do well together in the garden.

Herbs can greatly expand the potential of your garden. Fragrant herbs include: lemon verbena, various mints, pennyroyal, rosemary, and Sweet Annie. They not only provide fragrance, but also add taste to your meals, provide herbal remedies, and look attractive. Herbs can be used to give a delicate fragrance to your linen and clothes.[12] Your herb garden can be placed anywhere on your property, but the Family location is usually considered the best, as this area also relates to health. In chapter 8, we will discuss herb gardens in greater detail.

In past centuries, housewives made their own potpourri to help disguise the smell created by unwashed bodies and lack of sanitation. Nowadays, most people buy potpourri, but it is easy to make and is a wonderful personal gift to give to others. Remember that lavender, carnations, and roses are the only flowers that retain their scent after drying. Other flowers, such as cornflowers, delphiniums, and marigolds, are used in potpourri for their attractive colors. Flower oils and spices are often added to strengthen the fragrance.

Potpourri is highly positive from a feng shui point of view because the beautiful scents create ch'i and act as a remedy. However, they are made from *dried* flowers, which are considered negative. After all, feng shui means "wind and water," and dried flowers have had all the water removed. Consequently, some feng shui practitioners are opposed to the use of potpourri. This is understandable, but I feel that the fragrance and benefits that potpourri provides far outweigh the negative aspects of their production.

In past centuries, noblewomen would not venture outdoors without a nosegay of fragrant flowers called a Tussie Mussie (Figure 6B). These were believed to protect them from illness as well as the unpleasant odor of the street. These nosegays consisted of a small bouquet of flowers, chosen for color as well as scent. The term "Tussie

Mussie" dates back to at least 1440, and would doubtless be just as well known today if sanitation had not improved so much over the last 200 years.[13] In Victorian times, the selection of flowers in Tussie Mussies were used to exchange secret messages. This became so popular that many books were produced to explain the meanings of different flowers. One of the most popular of these books was Kate Greenaway's *The Illuminated Language of Flowers*, which is still available.[14]

Figure 6B: Tussie Mussie

Tussie Mussies are very easy to make. Select a range of scented flowers and foliage. Miniature roses, lavender, thyme, marjoram, pansies, sweet peas, lemon verbena, chamomile, and honeysuckle are all flowers that I have used for this purpose. Cut the stems to a suitable length and place them all in a vase for two to three hours. After this, you can create a posy by starting from the center and working outward, binding layer after layer of flowers into the bunch. Loosely bind the flowers together as you gather them, using raffia, wool, string, or thread. It is easier to do this if you rotate the posy in your hand as you add different flowers. Once the posy is of the desired size, finish it off with a circle of fragrant leaves. Ribbons and lace can be added if desired.

Tussie Mussies make a wonderful small gift that is unusual and appealing. You can also place them in different parts of your house to add color and fragrance.

You can plant perfumed flowers anywhere you wish in your garden. For instance, roses can improve your relationship if planted in the Marriage area. Choose the color with care. Pink roses represent a more idealistic, romantic love than red roses, which are fiery and passionate. The more fragrant they are, the better.

Inside the house, you can place freshly cut, scented flowers anywhere you wish. Potted plants also allow you the pleasure of scented flowers indoors. One particular pleasure of mine is enjoying the scent of the sweet-smelling spiky-leaved pelargonium on a cold winter's evening.

If you have an open fire, you can enjoy fragrances in the winter by burning cherry and apple logs. An elderly relative of mine used to make bundles of lavender and rosemary during the summer to burn in her fire during the winter months. She told me that in her childhood, her father would take embers of rosemary and lavender from room to room to sweeten the air.

Above all, use your intuition to decide what colors and scents you wish to have in your garden. Obviously, you will have to compromise depending on your geographical location and the amount of sun and shade your property has. My wife and I enjoy wandering through garden supply centers and frequently find ourselves drawn to a certain plant because of its color or scent. If we feel it will do well in our garden, we buy it. We have learned that by trusting our intuition, we seldom make a mistake.

7

Your Secret Garden

Consider the lilies of the field, how they grow;
they toil not, neither do they spin.

—Matthew 6:28,
The Sermon on the Mount

A secret garden is simply a quiet, reasonably private part
of your garden where you can relax and leave the problems of the world behind. Ideally, it is a place where you
will not be disturbed. It is like a retreat, where you can
commune with nature and restore your soul.

Usually, a secret garden is sheltered from cold winds
and prying eyes by fences, hedges, walls, or the side of a
house. A garden that is protected in this way can often
support a greater variety of plants than a more open garden, and for many people this is the greatest attraction.

There are a number of feng shui advantages of a secret garden. Because it is protected from cold winds, the conditions are better for anything you plant here. The lack of wind also makes it a more pleasant place to sit and relax. There are no problems with soil erosion or wind damage. Scented plants are at their best here because the perfume can linger. You can create an attractive balance of sunny and shady areas (yang and yin). It is often a simple matter to place a small fountain or pond inside a secret garden. This creates and encourages ch'i energy and makes the garden more comfortable and welcoming. It is also relatively easy to place a magic square over a secret area like this. This allows you to create a garden that is as feng shui perfect as possible, activating the areas in your life that you want to enhance.

A Brief History of Secret Gardens

Enclosed gardens have been popular for thousands of years. They were originally designed to protect and shelter *people* rather than plants. Even today, many people like the protection of high walls and hedges.

Courtyards became popular in Greek and Roman times, and are just as popular today in areas that enjoy a warm climate. In the Middle Ages, walled castles were common; they provided protection and defense for the local people. Inside these walls were gardens, planted to provide food and medicinal herbs.

Monasteries were usually surrounded by high walls too—not so much for protection against invasion, but to provide privacy and protection from the outside world. The monks tried to be as self-sufficient as possible, cultivating large gardens of vegetables, herbs, and grapes.

In the sixteenth century, secret gardens inside a larger garden were popular.[1] By the time the eighteenth century began, however, people were starting to pull walls down to allow their gardens to flow into the neighboring countryside.[2] Still, walls never totally disappeared since they provided protection from grazing animals.

In the nineteenth century, enclosed gardens made a comeback. The growing middle class wanted a small area of land that they could call their own around their homes. They wanted a private space to give them a necessary retreat from the busy everyday world.

Characteristics of the Secret Garden

The variety of materials that can be used to enclose a secret garden has increased enormously over the years. However, we still use a mixture of the general elements of walls, trellises, fences, hedges, and other tall plants—just as the ancient Romans did.

Naturally, a secret garden splits up the property, and this makes it intrinsically more interesting. Sadly, dull and unimaginative gardens are common. A simple way of avoiding this fate for your garden is to create an atmosphere of mystery. A secret garden, by its very nature, does this. It divides the garden into different areas, and frequently offers a tantalizing glimpse of what may be beyond a wall or hedge.

Size

Even the smallest of gardens can contain a private, secret area. A friend of mine has a secret garden that is only six feet square. As her entire back garden is only three times this size, she decided to use a low brick wall to separate the two areas. Consequently, the entire garden can be seen from inside the house and anywhere in the garden. This means that her "secret" garden is not actually secret at all. In practice, however, since she lives on her own, no one can see her when she is spending time in the secret part of her garden.

Location

Secret gardens are normally hidden away somewhere in the back garden. However, they can be situated anywhere at all. A friend of mine in France has a magnificent secret garden on the roof of his house. It is surrounded by trellises for privacy and protection from the prevailing wind. The trellises are covered with climbing roses. It is one of the most restful places I have ever been in.

A Place to Unwind

Someone I know has two large oak trees in his garden. They mark the boundaries of his secret garden. Whenever he is feeling stressed, he simply lies down on the grass between these two trees and allows them to drain away all of his tension.

"I feel completely different when I get up," he says. "I don't know what it is, but those trees revitalize me in some strange sort of way."

At one time, when he was facing some extreme business pressures, he took to sleeping between the two trees. He believes that they helped him keep calm, relaxed, and in control of the situation. I have not tried sleeping between two trees, but can attest to the benefits of hugging trees.[3]

We all need somewhere to relax and unwind. A small private garden is the ideal place to do this, as we can commune with nature, enjoy the fresh air, and generally restore ourselves.

Innovation

Interestingly, you can enjoy a secret garden even if you live in an apartment. A city dweller that I know uses a small, reasonably private corner of a nearby park. Although she does not grow her own plants or do any gardening there, she still looks after her secret garden by weeding it and removing any litter. She claims that city life would be unbearable without ready access to this place. In many respects, she is using the ancient Celtic tradition of caring for the area around a personal oracle tree.[4]

Another apartment dweller told me that he enjoys sitting on the floor of his studio apartment, surrounded by potted plants.

"Of course, I know that I'm really sitting on a rug," he told me. "But it's still peaceful and calm. I talk to my plants and they definitely respond."

Your Own Style Is the Right Style

In the last house we owned, my wife and I had a totally secret garden that could not be seen by anyone. Our secret garden is reasonably private where we are now, but, theoretically at least, our neighbors could look through the fence palings and see inside. The important thing, though, is not how private your secret garden is, but how safe and protected you feel when you are inside it.

Friends of ours have a conservatory attached to their house and this serves as their secret garden. Because it is always warm inside, they are able to grow tropical plants that add to their pleasure and make their secret garden seem exotic and mysterious.

Obviously, the perfect secret garden would be surrounded by attractive walls protecting a beautiful garden full of your favorite plants. There would be a pleasant, winding path through a grove of trees that led to the entrance. There would also be a natural pond in the center and the entire garden would be a haven for song birds, butterflies, and people seeking to rid themselves of the stress and strain of daily life.

In practice, my wife and I have a secret garden that is much simpler than that. Part of it is made up of a large deck. We have a variety of plants in pots and tubs. This allows us to change their positions to catch the sun as the seasons change. We also have a metal wind chime here. Its cheerful song reminds us that the ch'i is flowing throughout the garden. From the deck we can walk down a small ramp to a totally private area where my wife has a large selection of her favorite plants.

Because it is protected from the prevailing wind, we are able to grow plants there that would not survive anywhere else on our property. We have chosen plants with plenty of foliage to increase the feelings of seclusion and privacy. We do not yet have a pond there, but that is going to be our next major project.

Our secret garden is a pleasant place that is close to the house, but is totally private. In the summer months, it becomes, in effect, an extra room where my wife and I spend hours chatting and enjoying the long summer evenings. In the winter, it is just as attractive and is noticeably warmer than any other part of the garden. Consequently, given fine weather, we are able to use it the whole year round.

There are countless things that you can do with your secret garden. You may introduce statues, garden gnomes, a fountain, or some other focal point. We have a large potted cherry tree that catches everybody's attention as soon as they come into the secluded part of our secret garden. You shouldn't have too many focal points, however. Most average-sized gardens can sustain only one. Too many focal points make the garden appear fussy. It is hard to relax in such a garden.

A secret garden is also the perfect place for a gazebo, pergola, or arbor. In fact, these can often become the focal point of the garden.

Simplicity of Design

It is a good idea to keep the garden itself relatively simple. The purpose of your secret garden is to have a place to unwind and relax. You do not want to spend all your spare hours working in it. Honeysuckle, lavender, primroses, roses, and herbs are all examples of plants that thrive well in secret gardens—they do not need a large amount of work. Incorporate any existing trees or large shrubs into your garden. They can provide dappled shade as well as privacy.

Choose colors that activate the different aspects of your life that you want to enhance. Plant them in the correct areas of your secret garden using the compass directions and the Aspirations of the pa-kua. Pay special attention to the plants that you have in your secret garden in this regard. Be aware of how they relate to the pa-kua and to activating areas of your life.

We become what we think about, and if, for example, you have planted pink roses in the Relationship sector, you will attract love and romance into your life. This will come about whether you think about it or not, but by making the pink roses a type of silent affirmation, you are also generating the right pattern of thoughts in your mind.

Use yin and yang by incorporating sunlight and shade and a mixture of short and tall plants. Also, be sure to incorporate complements to your personal element in the design.

Your secret garden can help you achieve everything you want. Treat it with respect, tend it, and spend as many quiet, relaxing hours in it as you can.

8

A Feng Shui Herb Garden

Here's flowers for you;

Hot lavender, mints, savory, marjoram;

The marigold, that goes to bed wi' the sun,

And with him rises weeping . . .

—William Shakespeare,
The Winter's Tale, iv, 111, 103

Herbs are the most sensuous of plants. Their pleasant fla-
vors and scents arouse profound memories in virtually
everyone. Herb gardens create large amounts of ch'i—
they provide color, fragrance, and sound. Just think of the
steady hum of bumblebees exploring your flowers.

Let us assume that you are about to create a small herb
garden. For the purposes of this example, we will use the
Aspirations of the pa-kua. In your own garden, of course,
you can place your herb garden in the right location
using your individually determined directions of the
compass in addition to the Aspirations.

Our imaginary garden will be just nine feet by nine feet, which allows three square feet for each of the different life activities revealed by the pa-kua.

We want the garden to look attractive, and also provide a variety of herbs that can be used in the kitchen or for making essential oils and herbal bouquets.

Choosing Herbs to Plant

Start by deciding which herbs you wish to plant. This should be done in terms of which herbs you are most likely to use as well as which ones will provide you with the colors and fragrances you require to activate different areas of the pa-kua. You also need to determine which herbs will grow best in your particular climate and soil conditions. Basil, for instance, comes from the Mediterranean, and needs plenty of sunlight and a warm climate to perform well. Catnip comes from Eurasia and enjoys a light shade. Here is a list of some useful herbs to consider for your garden:

Aloe. Produces a gel that can be used as a remedy for acne, burns, and abrasions.

Artemesia. Also known as *southernwood, Old Man* and *Lad's Love*. An ornamental herb that repels aphids and insects.

Basil. The highly scented leaves of this plant are used for culinary, medicinal, and cosmetic purposes.

Bee balm. Sometimes called *bergamot*. A mint with culinary properties, it has attractive red or pink flowers and a strong scent. Some Native American tribes used it to make a refreshing herbal tea. Allow plenty of room for bee balm; it spreads as it grows.

Borage. This is a bushy annual with bright blue flowers. The bristly leaves and seeds can be used as a compress.

Catnip. Sometimes called *catmint*. It can help relieve colds and fevers. It grows to almost two feet tall and produces beautiful, bright blue flowers.

Chamomile. It can be used in a variety of medicinal ways, such as helping people to sleep. The flowers of chamomile look like small daisies and produce an attractive, fruity scent.

Chives. A culinary herb with grass-like leaves that can add spice to any dish. It produces purple flowers in the late spring.

Comfrey. This herb can take over the garden if not kept in check. It produces white, blue and purple flowers. It is helpful for many skin problems.

Coriander. This plant looks like parsley, but the leaves have a distinctive, tangy taste. It is frequently used in potpourri.

Dandelion. The dandelion is often considered to be a weed, but it makes an excellent diuretic and blood tonic.

Dill. A culinary herb with soft, feathery leaves. Do not plant it next to fennel, as each adversely affects the flavor of the other.

Echinacea. A medicinal herb with purple flowers. It makes an excellent blood purifier.

Fennel. This herb can be used for a variety of purposes, both culinary and medicinal.

Garlic. The "wonder herb." Garlic can be used for culinary and medicinal purposes.

Lavender. This plant produces a fresh scent that is instantly recognizable. The beautiful mauve flowers are used in potpourri and lavender bottles. A lavender bag in the bedroom can help people to sleep better.

Lemon balm. A culinary herb that creates positive feelings. It produces tiny white flowers and lemon-perfumed, heart-shaped leaves. It also attracts bees to the garden.

Lemon verbena. This citrus-scented plant has attractive, crinkly, narrow leaves. It makes a beautiful lemon tea, and is also used for cosmetics and potpourri.

Marjoram. A fragrant herb that produces beautiful pink or purple flowers. It has a delicate scent that is used in potpourri.

Mint. An essential herb that should be in every garden. There are many types of mint to choose from. The most popular perfumed mints are apple mint, peppermint, pineapple and spearmint.

Oregano. A culinary herb that can also be used for medicinal purposes. The variety with the strongest flavor is Greek oregano.

Parsley. A culinary herb that also makes an excellent deodorant.

Rosemary. A culinary and medicinal herb with tiny blue flowers. It is used as a cure for headaches and rheumatism.

Sage. Sage has gray leaves and delicate blue flowers. It is a useful herb for medicinal, culinary, and beauty purposes.

Thyme. A culinary and antiseptic herb. There are many varieties of thyme and the color of the flowers varies anywhere from white to violet. Sprigs of thyme in the wardrobe or drawers will repel fleas and moths. In ancient times, the Greeks and Romans burned thyme to eliminate offensive odors and make public places·smell fresh.[1]

Yarrow. This has been considered a healing herb for thousands of years. It has small pink or white flowers and a distinctive, spicy scent.

There are many others to choose from, but those listed above are arguably the most useful herbs for a small garden. Decide which herbs you want to use and find out how much room each herb will require. It is not good feng shui for your herbs to be fighting for space.

Placement of Herbs in the Garden

I find it helpful to place each herb on the lawn beside the garden and change them around until I am happy with their positions. I do this using my feelings, aesthetic judgment, the Aspirations of the pa-kua, and the compass directions. I will probably place the perfumed herbs around the edges of the garden to make it easier for me to savor their scents. Most herbs need to be crushed or rubbed to release their aroma, so it is preferable to have them within easy reach.

Naturally, I also take into consideration how large the plants will become. Taller plants may interfere with smaller ones. Angelica, for example, can grow up to seven feet in height. Plants that spread will overpower neighboring plants.

I must additionally consider whether the plant is an annual or perennial. All of this may sound complicated, but in practice, it is easy—I will have checked the height, spread, environmental needs, and other characteristics of each herb before buying it in the first place.

There is no correct way of choosing positions in the herb garden, but I find it helpful to do it in the way I've just described. After all, it is much less work to decide their final positions *before* planting rather than trying to do so *while* you plant or even afterward.

I normally make my decisions and then go away for an hour or two. This allows my subconscious mind to work on the correct placements while I am thinking about other things. I usually make a few changes when I return. I do this as many times as necessary. Once I have come back and made no changes, I am ready to transfer them to their new home in the ground.

Several people I know ignore the aesthetics and plant their herbs using the Aspirations of the pa-kua as their sole guide. This works for them, but I want my garden to look as attractive as possible, also. Beneficial ch'i is created whenever anything is beautiful. I want my herb garden to be beautiful as well as functional.

Even if you decide to work out a design based purely on the Aspirations of the pa-kua, you have a number of decisions to make. You may, for instance, decide to plant bee balm in the Wealth area because you feel that its scarlet flowers will provide the necessary motivation to help you progress financially. This would especially be the case if you belonged to the Earth element, as Fire (red) creates Earth in the productive cycle of elements (see page 15). Another person might plant it in the Family area to activate the health and physical fitness of a family member. Someone else might decide to ignore the pa-kua and use bee balm purely for its delightful mint and citrus flavor. Another person might plant it to attract butterflies.

There are probably thousands of reasons people choose to plant bee balm in their garden. You'll need to consider all of your options in light of your own desires as well as feng shui principles, then make the appropriate judgment for your situation.

Herb gardens can also reflect your personal interests. Years ago, I saw a Shakespearean herb garden that someone had created using only herbs that Shakespeare wrote about. This made for an attractive herb garden that also provided the owner with pleasant thoughts about Shakespeare's plays whenever he looked at it. Other people have created similar gardens using plants named after gods or people's names.[2]

9

Taking Your Garden Indoors

I remember being amazed when a friend told me that she took her garden indoors for the winter. She lived in a cold climate and her plants would not survive outside during the long winter months. The practical solution was to have plenty of potted plants that could be brought inside when the cold was too severe.

I have always enjoyed having plants indoors as well as out. In our home, we have a number of potted plants that are used for aesthetic as well as feng shui purposes. We also have a regular supply of freshly cut flowers for much of the year. Cut flowers are attractive and provide both color and fragrance, but it is important that they be removed as soon as they start to die. Dead flowers create negative, or shar, ch'i. Dried flowers are also bad from a feng shui point of view, though we make an exception for potpourri. As you will recall, feng shui means "wind and water," and dried flowers have no water.

Potted plants and cut flowers are the most obvious ways that we can bring the garden indoors. Of course, if you are fortunate enough to have a conservatory, you can bring an entire garden inside, but few of us are in the position to do that.

Before we had an outdoor herb garden, my wife and I had a small one on the window ledge of our kitchen. It was tiny, but it looked attractive and produced an abundance of fresh herbs.

Our first home was an apartment. Consequently, our entire garden was a small window box. Despite its size, it gave us great pleasure. The colorful displays we produced in it created beneficial ch'i and enlivened our small home. Whenever I think back to those days, our tiny window box garden comes to mind. You do not necessarily need an outdoor garden to put the ideas of this book into practice.

How to Increase Ch'i with Scent and Color

Fortunately, there are many ways to bring the colors and fragrances of our gardens inside. Place flowers of the colors that represent different members of your household around the house. They become silent affirmations—whenever you see them, they will remind you of the special people in your life.

Use fragrances anywhere you wish. The "good luck center" of the house is a beneficial place because from there, the fragrance will be able to spread throughout every part of your home.

Tussie Mussies (chapter 6) are a good example of using color and scent to increase positive ch'i. Several other useful examples follow.

Herbs

Herbs can be taken indoors. They provide a wonderful and useful display in the kitchen. Herb bags make useful gifts, and herbal baths are refreshing and beneficial.

Pomanders

Pomanders made from oranges that are studded with cloves create a spicy scent. They make a striking and unusual gift. Pomanders can also be made from lemons, limes, and green apples.

Potpourri

Potpourri, despite being controversial from a feng shui point of view, allows the scents of the garden to be present indoors all year round. Potpourri can also be put into small bags of material and placed anywhere around the house. A lady I know places these bags among her cushions. Whenever someone sits down on her lounge suite, they are greeted with a beautiful scent.

Bags of potpourri and herbs can also be placed in wardrobes to keep clothes smelling fresh and to deter insects. Too, they can be placed beneath the pillow to ensure a restful sleep. There is no limit to where potpourri can be used. I have seen hanging mobiles stuffed with potpourri. Recently, my wife and I stayed in a hotel where the covered coat hangers were filled with a fragrant potpourri.

Perfumed Water

Before the days of running water, perfumed water was frequently used for cleaning one's face and hands. Perfumed flower petals would be placed into jugs of water overnight to keep the water fresh until morning. Perfumed water can still be used today to provide a sense of extravagance and indulgence at no cost.

Shampoos and Conditioners

Shampoos and conditioners that are made from herbs tend to be more gentle than commercial products. Lemon balm makes a wonderful shampoo. Its fragrance makes washing your hair a delightful experience. Chamomile makes an excellent conditioner for light-colored hair. Sage is better for people with darker hair.

Toilet Water

Toilet water, a scented water with a high alcohol level, is refreshing and revitalizing. It first became popular with the ladies in waiting at the court of Queen Elizabeth I and rapidly grew in popularity thereafter.

Eau de Cologne. Eau de Cologne was introduced in 1725 by an innovative Italian who lived in Cologne. It is still the most famous toilet water.

Carmelite Water. Carmelite water was invented by Carmelite monks in 1611. It is one of the easiest toilet waters to make. You need half a pint of good quality vodka, six tablespoons of chopped angelica leaves and stalks, six tablespoons of chopped lemon balm leaves, half an ounce of bruised coriander seeds, one chopped nutmeg, two tablespoons of cloves, and four one-inch pieces of cinnamon stick.

All the ingredients are placed in a jar and shaken vigorously. The jar needs to be kept in a warm place. Shake it every day. After three weeks, the carmelite water is strained out and rebottled. It can be used immediately.

Scented Candles and Vaporizers

Scented candles have been used for thousands of years to perfume rooms. Vaporizers have also become popular in recent years. A vaporizer is a ceramic container that allows a small candle flame to gently heat essential oil, causing the oil to vaporize and thereby scent the room.

Candlemaking. Candles are easy to make, as long as you have the proper materials. If you try to make candles from kitchen paraffin and crayons, for instance, you are likely to be disappointed—the candles you produce will probably be smoky, dangerously hot, or produce an unpleasant smell.

Proper materials can be found at most craft stores. Buy candle paraffin, stearic acid (to make the paraffin tough and to help it burn evenly), wicks, coloring materials, and molds. You will be able to buy scents that have been specially prepared for candles there, as well. These specially prepared scents will hold their aroma for a longer period of time than scents that aren't made specifically for candles. They are made of pure oil.

Aromatherapy oils can be used to scent candles as well. However, since many of these have medicinal properties, you should read some books on aromatherapy before experimenting with them. Any *oil-based* scent can be used, but it pays to experiment with different types and quantities to achieve the best results. You should avoid anything that has an alcohol or water base.

You can experiment in other ways as well. Aromatic spices added to the wax before pouring create interesting scents. Crushed flowers are inclined to settle in the wax, but they do create beautiful fragrances.

To make your candles, use a double boiler and ensure that you work in a well-ventilated area. A bowl and a saucepan can make an impromptu double boiler, if necessary. Remember, wax can ignite if overheated, and different waxes ignite at different temperatures. You should make yourself aware of the properties of whatever wax you are using, and then use a thermometer to keep track of temperature. It pays to be cautious when making candles, since hot wax can inflict unpleasant burns.

Make sure that your molds are clean and dry. Virtually anything that will withstand the heat of melted wax can be used as a mold. If you are using a commercial mold, spray it with a silicone spray or oil it with vegetable oil to allow easy removal of the candle once it has set. Melt the candle paraffin in the double boiler and then add the stearic acid (one part acid to ten parts wax). Do *not* let this mixture get hotter than 200 degrees Fahrenheit. Carefully pour or ladle the mixture into a jug, then stir in the coloring. Center a rod over the mold and attach the candle wick to it. You may need to weight the wick's end to ensure that it remains in contact with the bottom of the mold. Next, pour the wax into the mold. Pour as close to the center of the mold as you can—this will help to ensure that you avoid making bubbles.

Add the scent to the mold immediately after pouring the wax. Follow the fragrance manufacturer's instructions for the correct quantity of scent. The usual amount is one half ounce of scent per pound of wax. Allow the candle to harden for at least an hour at 70 degrees Fahrenheit. When it has set, tap the sides of the mold and then dip it briefly in hot water to release the candle. Trim the wick to about half an inch in length.

If desired, you can add a small amount of beeswax to the mixture at the same time as you are adding the stearic acid. This raises the melting point of the wax, making your candle last longer. Also, beeswax produces a delightful scent when the candle is burned.

Keep your scented candles in a plastic bag until they are ready to be used. They tend to lose their fragrance if kept unprotected for any length of time. There are many books available at craft and book stores that provide further detailed instructions on making candles.

Aromatic Fire

Many herbs perfume the room if they are placed on an open fire. Lavender, angelica and rosemary are good examples. Aromatic woods, such as cypress and juniper, were used to scent rooms in the sixteenth to nineteenth centuries. Superstitions developed about some of these. For instance, rosemary and bay leaves were believed to ward off evil spirits, while southernwood would deter any "serpents lurking in the corners." It was also believed to be an omen of death if you could smell flowers when none were present.[1]

Fir and pine cones create a pleasant scent as they burn. However, they can also be used to create a pleasing fragrance *before* you burn them. Put a few drops of an herb or spice oil on each one and place them close to the fire. As the room heats up, the cones will release a pleasant perfume.

Conclusion

Life should be a beautiful, joyful experience for us all. By consciously adding beauty, color, and fragrance to our environment, we make our lives happier and brighter in every way. In the process, we also create an abundance of ch'i, making our home a harmonious place to live.

The Chinese believe that if you are surrounded by an abundance of ch'i, you will lead a life rich in happiness, contentment, and abundance. If your life is not currently full of these things, look around your garden using feng shui as a guide. Eliminate or repel any shars, clear out the clutter, do any necessary repairs, and plant more flowers.

I hope this book will inspire you to look at your garden with new eyes, and to make any changes that will increase the amount of ch'i that comes into your home.

It is best to make one or two changes at a time, and then wait a few weeks before making more. This gradual process gives you the opportunity to experience and evaluate the effects of each change.

I am confident that once you have feng shuied your garden and experienced the beneficial effects it creates, you will want to feng shui your home and work environments as well. I wish you a life rich in happiness, contentment, and abundance.

Appendix

Elements and Signs for the Years 1900 to 2000

Element	Sign	Year
Metal	Rat	Jan. 31, 1900 to Feb. 18, 1901
Metal	Ox	Feb. 19, 1901 to Feb. 7, 1902
Water	Tiger	Feb. 8, 1902 to Jan. 28, 1903
Water	Rabbit	Jan. 29, 1903 to Feb. 15, 1904
Wood	Dragon	Feb. 16, 1904 to Feb. 3, 1905
Wood	Snake	Feb. 4, 1905 to Jan. 24, 1906
Fire	Horse	Jan. 25, 1906 to Feb. 12, 1907
Fire	Sheep	Feb. 13, 1907 to Feb. 1, 1908
Earth	Monkey	Feb. 2, 1908 to Jan. 21, 1909
Earth	Rooster	Jan. 22, 1909 to Feb. 9, 1910
Metal	Dog	Feb. 10, 1910 to Jan. 29, 1911
Metal	Boar	Jan. 30, 1911 to Feb. 17, 1912
Water	Rat	Feb. 18, 1912 to Feb. 5, 1913
Water	Ox	Feb. 6, 1913 to Jan. 25, 1914
Wood	Tiger	Jan. 26, 1914 to Feb. 13, 1915

Wood	Rabbit	Feb. 14, 1915 to Feb. 2, 1916
Fire	Dragon	Feb. 3, 1916 to Jan. 22, 1917
Fire	Snake	Jan. 23, 1917 to Feb. 10, 1918
Earth	Horse	Feb. 11, 1918 to Jan. 31, 1919
Earth	Sheep	Feb. 1, 1919 to Feb. 19, 1920
Metal	Monkey	Feb. 20, 1920 to Feb. 7, 1921
Metal	Rooster	Feb. 8, 1921 to Jan. 27, 1922
Water	Dog	Jan. 28, 1922 to Feb. 15, 1923
Water	Boar	Feb. 16, 1923 to Feb. 4, 1924
Wood	Rat	Feb. 5, 1924 to Jan. 24, 1925
Wood	Ox	Jan. 25, 1925 to Feb. 12, 1926
Fire	Tiger	Feb. 13, 1926 to Feb. 1, 1927
Fire	Rabbit	Feb. 2, 1927 to Jan. 22, 1928
Earth	Dragon	Jan. 23, 1928 to Feb. 9, 1929
Earth	Snake	Feb. 10, 1929 to Jan. 29, 1930
Metal	Horse	Jan. 30, 1930 to Feb. 16, 1931
Metal	Sheep	Feb. 17, 1931 to Feb. 5, 1932
Water	Monkey	Feb. 6, 1932 to Jan. 25, 1933
Water	Rooster	Jan. 26, 1933 to Feb. 13, 1934
Wood	Dog	Feb. 14, 1934 to Feb. 3, 1935
Wood	Boar	Feb. 4, 1935 to Jan. 23, 1936
Fire	Rat	Jan. 24, 1936 to Feb. 10, 1937
Fire	Ox	Feb. 11, 1937 to Jan. 30, 1938
Earth	Tiger	Jan. 31, 1938 to Feb. 18, 1939
Earth	Rabbit	Feb. 19, 1939 to Feb. 7, 1940
Metal	Dragon	Feb. 8, 1940 to Jan. 26, 1941
Metal	Snake	Jan. 27, 1941 to Feb. 14, 1942
Water	Horse	Feb. 15, 1942 to Feb. 4, 1943
Water	Sheep	Feb. 5, 1943 to Jan. 24, 1944

Wood	Monkey	Jan. 25, 1944 to Feb. 12, 1945
Wood	Rooster	Feb. 13, 1945 to Feb. 1, 1946
Fire	Dog	Feb. 2, 1946 to Jan. 21, 1947
Fire	Boar	Jan. 22, 1947 to Feb. 9, 1948
Earth	Rat	Feb. 10, 1948 to Jan. 28, 1949
Earth	Ox	Jan. 29, 1949 to Feb. 16, 1950
Metal	Tiger	Feb. 17, 1950 to Feb. 5, 1951
Metal	Rabbit	Feb. 6, 1951 to Jan. 26, 1952
Water	Dragon	Jan. 27, 1952 to Feb. 13, 1953
Water	Snake	Feb. 14, 1953 to Feb. 2, 1954
Wood	Horse	Feb. 3, 1954 to Jan. 23, 1955
Wood	Sheep	Jan. 24, 1955 to Feb. 11, 1956
Fire	Monkey	Feb. 12, 1956 to Jan. 30, 1957
Fire	Rooster	Jan. 31, 1957 to Feb. 17, 1958
Earth	Dog	Feb. 18, 1958 to Feb. 7, 1959
Earth	Boar	Feb. 8, 1959 to Jan. 27, 1960
Metal	Rat	Jan. 28, 1960 to Feb. 14, 1961
Metal	Ox	Feb. 15, 1961 to Feb. 4, 1962
Water	Tiger	Feb. 5, 1962 to Jan. 24, 1963
Water	Rabbit	Jan. 25, 1963 to Feb. 12, 1964
Wood	Dragon	Feb. 13, 1964 to Feb. 1, 1965
Wood	Snake	Feb. 2, 1965 to Jan. 20, 1966
Fire	Horse	Jan. 21, 1966 to Feb. 8, 1967
Fire	Sheep	Feb. 9, 1967 to Jan. 29, 1968
Earth	Monkey	Jan. 30, 1968 to Feb. 16, 1969
Earth	Rooster	Feb. 17, 1969 to Feb. 5, 1970
Metal	Dog	Feb. 6, 1970 to Jan. 26, 1971
Metal	Boar	Jan. 27, 1971 to Jan. 15, 1972
Water	Rat	Jan. 16, 1972 to Feb. 2, 1973

Water	Ox	Feb. 3, 1973 to Jan. 22, 1974
Wood	Tiger	Jan. 23, 1974 to Feb. 10, 1975
Wood	Rabbit	Feb. 11, 1975 to Jan. 30, 1976
Fire	Dragon	Jan. 31, 1976 to Feb. 17, 1977
Fire	Snake	Feb. 18, 1977 to Feb. 6, 1978
Earth	Horse	Feb. 7, 1978 to Jan. 27, 1979
Earth	Sheep	Jan. 28, 1979 to Feb. 15, 1980
Metal	Monkey	Feb. 16, 1980 to Feb. 4, 1981
Metal	Rooster	Feb. 5, 1981 to Jan. 24, 1982
Water	Dog	Jan. 25, 1982 to Feb. 12, 1983
Water	Boar	Feb. 13, 1983 to Feb. 1, 1984
Wood	Rat	Feb. 2, 1984 to Feb. 19, 1985
Wood	Ox	Feb. 20, 1985 to Feb. 8, 1986
Fire	Tiger	Feb. 9, 1986 to Jan. 28, 1987
Fire	Rabbit	Jan. 29, 1987 to Feb. 16, 1988
Earth	Dragon	Feb. 17, 1988 to Feb. 5, 1989
Earth	Snake	Feb. 6, 1989 to Jan. 26, 1990
Metal	Horse	Jan. 27, 1990 to Feb. 14, 1991
Metal	Sheep	Feb. 15, 1991 to Feb. 3, 1992
Water	Monkey	Feb. 4, 1992 to Jan. 22, 1993
Water	Rooster	Jan. 23, 1993 to Feb. 9, 1994
Wood	Dog	Feb. 10, 1994 to Jan. 30, 1995
Wood	Boar	Jan. 31, 1995 to Feb. 18, 1996
Fire	Rat	Feb. 19, 1996 to Feb. 6, 1997
Fire	Ox	Feb. 7, 1997 to Jan. 27, 1998
Earth	Tiger	Jan. 28, 1998 to Feb. 15, 1999
Earth	Rabbit	Feb. 16, 1999 to Feb. 4, 2000
Metal	Dragon	Feb. 5, 2000

Notes

Introduction

1. Ficino, Marsilio. *Marsilio Ficino: The Book of Life*. Translated by Charles Boer. Dallas: Spring Publications, 1980, page 134.
2. William Blake, quoted in *Unfolding Seasons* by Kerry Carman. Auckland: Random Century New Zealand Limited, 1992, page 122.
3. Whiten, Faith and Geoff. *Chinese Garden Style*. London: Unwin Hyman Limited, 1988, page 57.

Chapter One

1. Bloomfield, Frena, *The Book of Chinese Beliefs*. London: Arrow Books Limited, 1983, page 21.
2. Peterson, Russell. "At Last, Earth's Future is a Truly Global Concern." Article in L.A. Times, May 14th, 1989.
3. Diamond, Harvey. *Your Heart, Your Planet*. Santa Monica, CA: Hay House Inc., 1990, page 96.

Chapter Two

1. Allardice, Pamela. *Green Thumbs*. Sydney: Bay Books, 1994, page 124.

Chapter Three

1. Chiu, T. N. and C. L. So, ed. *A Geography of Hong Kong*. Hong Kong: Oxford University Press, 1983, pages 59–62.

2. Too, Lillian. *The Complete Illustrated Guide to Feng Shui*. Longmead: Element Books Limited, 1996, page 206.

Chapter Six

1. The most accessible of the modern books on color psychology is *The Beginner's Guide to Colour Psychology* by Angela Wright (London: Kyle Cathie Limited, 1995). The most influential of the earlier books on the subject is *Color Psychology and Color Therapy* by Faber Birren (Secaucus, NJ: Citadel Press, 1950).

2. Mella, Dorothee L. *The Language of Color*. New York: Viking Penguin, Inc., 1988, page 9.

3. Isaacs, Jennifer. *The Secret Meaning of Flowers*. East Roseville, Australia: Simon and Schuster Australia, 1993, page 93.

4. Wright, Angela. *The Beginner's Guide to Colour Psychology*. London: Kyle Cathie Limited, 1995, page 82.

5. Hessayon, Dr. D. G. *The Armchair Book of the Garden*. London: Century Publishing Co. Ltd., 1983, page 45.

6. Many people are confused about which flowers are geraniums and which are pelargoniums. "Geranium" is the term that is usually used to describe the family of plants called *geraniaceae*, which includes pelargoniums. In fact, most of the plants that are called "geraniums" are actually pelargoniums.

7. The prophet Mohammed, quoted in *Green Thumbs* by Pamela Allardice. Sydney: Bay Books, 1994, page 130.

8. *Encyclopaedia Britannica, Micropaedia.* Chicago: Encyclopaedia Britannica, Inc., fifteenth edition, 1983, vol. vii, page 872.

9. Carman, Kerry. *Unfolding Seasons.* Auckland: Random Century New Zealand Limited, 1992, page 41.

10. Abraham, Doc and Katy. *Green Thumb Wisdom.* Pownal, VT: Storey Communications, Inc., 1996, pages 33–34.

11. Allardice, Pamela. *Green Thumbs.* Sydney: Bay Books, 1994, page 92.

12. Griffin, Judy, Ph.D. *Mother Nature's Herbal.* St. Paul, MN: Llewellyn, 1997, page 114. Judy Griffin also describes an attractive fragrant garden on page 265.

13. Dunn, Olive. *Delights of a Fragrant Garden.* Auckland, NZ: Century Hutchinson New Zealand Limited, 1989, page 73.

14. Greenaway, Kate. *The Illuminated Language of Flowers.* London: Macdonald and Jane's, 1887. Reprinted 1978. At least 150 flower dictionaries were published in Victorian times, attesting to the popularity of flowers as a means of exchanging secret messages in a time when young couples were never without a chaperone. It must have been devastating to see an anenome,

which means "refusal." How exciting, though, to see a gardenia ("secret love"), foxglove ("sincerity"), or cinnamon ("everything I own is yours").

Chapter Seven

1. Stevens, David and Ursula Buchan. *The Ultimate Garden Book for North America.* New York: Rizzoli International Publications, Inc., 1996, page 46.
2. Toogood, Alan. *The Sheltered Garden.* Newton Abbot: David and Charles Publishers pic, 1989, page 16.
3. Webster, Richard. *Seven Secrets to Success.* St. Paul: Llewellyn Publications, 1997.
4. Webster, Richard. *Omens, Oghams and Oracles.* St. Paul: Llewellyn Publications, 1995, pages 39–41.

Chapter Eight

1. Duff, Gail. *Natural Fragrances.* London: Sidgwick and Jackson Limited, 1989, page 13.
2. Clayton, Fay. *Deities in My Garden.* Paraparaumu, New Zealand: Ety Publications, 1994, and Clayton, Fay. *Gentlemen in my Garden.* Paraparaumu, New Zealand: Ety Publications, 1992.

Chapter Nine

1. Zolar. *Zolar's Encyclopedia of Omens, Signs and Superstitions.* New York: Prentice Hall Press, 1989), page 310.

Glossary

Ch'i — Ch'i is the universal life force that is found in all living things. It is created by anything beautiful and when anything is done perfectly. The perfect place to site your home is where there is an abundance of ch'i. Traditionally, this would be a south-facing site, protected by hills behind and with gently flowing water in front.

Compass School — This is one of the two main schools of feng shui. The other is the Form school. The Compass school uses the degrees of the compass and the details of the person's date of birth to determine his or her positive and negative directions. In practice, most feng shui practitioners use a combination of both the Form and Compass schools when making their assessments.

Cycle of Destruction — The five elements can be arranged in an order where each element overpowers

137

and dominates the element that follows it in the cycle. In the Cycle of Destruction: Fire melts and destroys metal. Metal can destroy wood. Wood draws its energy from the earth. Earth can block up and dam water. Water can put out fire.

Cycle of Production — The five elements can be placed in a number of arrangements. In the Cycle of Production (also frequently known as the Cycle of Birth) each element assists and supports the element that follows it in the cycle. In this cycle: Wood burns and creates fire. Fire produces earth. From the earth comes metal. Metal liquifies, symbolizing water. Finally, water nurtures and nourishes wood.

Feng Shui — Feng shui literally means "wind and water." It is the art of living in harmony with your environment. In feng shui it is believed that by choosing the right locations to live and work, you will lead a life of happiness, contentment, and abundance. Feng shui has a history that goes back thousands of years into Chinese pre-history. During the twentieth century it has spread around the world, and is more popular today than ever before.

Five Elements — The five traditional elements of Chinese astrology are used in feng shui, and everything is believed to be composed of these elements. The five elements (wood, fire, earth, metal and water) each have their own distinct energy. The five elements can be arranged in a number of ways. In feng shui we use both the Cycle of Production and the Cycle of Destruction.

Form School — This is the older of two main schools of feng shui. The other is the Compass school. The Form school looks at the geography of the landscape to determine which locations produce the most ch'i. These are the best places to build a home.

I Ching — The I Ching, often called "The Book of Changes," is the oldest book of China, and is believed to have been created by Wu of Hsia in 3322 B.C.E. The I Ching has had a profound effect on Chinese history and culture. For thousands of years scholars, emperors and generals have consulted it to gain insight before making important decisions. The I Ching is the only book that was spared when Chin Shih-Huang ordered all the books in China to be destroyed in 215 B.C.E. It is an oracle consisting of sixty-four symbols known as hexagrams. Each hexagram consists of two trigrams, one placed on top of the other to create a six-lined figure. These hexagrams can be used for both divination and meditation.

Magic Square — A magic square consists of a series of numbers arranged inside a grid where all the horizontal, vertical and diagonal lines add up to the same total. In the West, magic squares are regarded simply as a branch of recreational mathematics, but in the East they are considered to have many magical properties. Feng shui derives from a magic square that Wu of Hsia found on the back of a tortoise shell. This same magic square also formed the basis of the I Ching, Chinese astrology, Chinese numerology, the Ki and Kigaku.

Pa-kua — The pa-kua is usually found hanging over the doors of Chinese households as a protective talisman and symbol of protection. It is octagonal in shape and usually contains either a mirror or yin-yang symbol in the center. Around this are displayed the eight trigrams from the I Ching. The pa-kua indicates the eight compass directions. The trigrams are all related to the five elements. Consequently, by using the pa-kua we can determine a person's positive and negative directions.

Remedies — Remedies are any devices used to eliminate the potentially harmful effects of shars or imbalances in the five elements. For instance, a hedge or fence could serve as a remedy for a shar coming from a neighboring house.

Secret Garden — A secret garden is a place where you can sit and relax in quiet, peaceful surroundings. Ideally, you will feel safe, comfortable and relaxed in a secret garden. Naturally, the garden will need to be looked after, but its purpose is to provide a private, tranquil environment where you can simply relax and become in tune with nature.

Shars — Shars, which are frequently referred to as "poison arrows," are negative energies that carry the potential for bad luck. Shars are straight lines that are created in a variety of ways. A straight road heading directly towards your house, as in a T-junction, is a major shar. An angle created by two walls of a neighboring house might create an arrow that points directly towards you. This is also a shar. Fortunately, there are remedies for almost every shar.

Trigrams — The eight trigrams from the I Ching comprise every possible combination of straight and broken lines that can be constructed from three lines. The straight lines are called yang lines and represent masculine energy. The broken lines are called yin lines and represent feminine energy. The trigrams are believed to have been created by Wu of Hsia and contain all the wisdom of the universe.

Wu of Hsia — Wu of Hsia (sometimes referred to as Fu Hsi) was the first ruler of China and is believed to have lived some 4,800 years ago. The Chinese had five mythical emperors, each of whom is credited with inventing something. Wu is credited with inventing feng shui, the I Ching, Chinese astrology and Chinese numerology. No one knows if any of the five mythical emperors actually existed.

Yin and Yang — Yin and yang are the two opposites in Taoist philosophy. Neither is capable of living without the other. For instance, front and back are two opposites. Without a front, there could be no back. Yin and yang have never been explicitly defined, but even today the Chinese people delight in coming up with lists of opposites to represent them. Yin is female, while yang is male. The opposite sides of a mountain are believed to have led to the creation of this concept; the shady northern side is called yin while the sunny southern side is called yang. This dualistic view of the universe plays an important role in feng shui. In our gardens, we want to achieve a balance of yin and yang to create the sense of a harmonious whole.

Suggested Reading

Abraham, Doc and Katy. *Green Thumb Wisdom*. Pownal, VT: Storey Communications, Inc., 1996.

Bloomfield, Frena. *The Book of Chinese Beliefs*. London, UK: Arrow Books Limited, 1983.

Griffin, Judy. *Mother Nature's Herbal*. St. Paul, MN: Llewellyn Publications, 1997.

Park, Polly. *The World in my Garden*. Kenthurst, Australia: Kangaroo Press, Pty. Limited, 1988.

Stein, Sara. *Noah's Garden: Restoring the Ecology of Our Own Back Yards*. New York: Houghton Mifflin Company, 1993.

Stevens, David and Ursula Buchan. *The Ultimate Garden Book for North America*. New York: Rizzoli International Publications, Inc., 1996.

Webster, Richard. *Feng Shui for Beginners*. St. Paul, MN: Llewellyn Publications, 1997.

Whiten, Faith and Geoff. *Chinese Garden Style*. London, UK: Unwin Hyman Limited, 1988.

Index

☽ LOOK FOR THE CRESCENT MOON

Llewellyn publishes hundreds of books on your favorite subjects! To get these exciting books, including the ones on the following pages, check your local bookstore or order them directly from Llewellyn.

ORDER BY PHONE

- Call toll-free within the U.S. and Canada, 1-800-THE MOON
- In Minnesota, call (612) 291-1970
- We accept VISA, MasterCard, and American Express

ORDER BY MAIL

- Send the full price of your order (MN residents add 7% sales tax) in U.S. funds, plus postage & handling to:

  Llewellyn Worldwide
  P.O. Box 64383, Dept. K793-5
  St. Paul, MN 55164–0383, U.S.A.

POSTAGE & HANDLING

(For the U.S., Canada, and Mexico)

- $4.00 for orders $15.00 and under
- $5.00 for orders over $15.00
- No charge for orders over $100.00

We ship UPS in the continental United States. We ship standard mail to P.O. boxes. Orders shipped to Alaska, Hawaii, The Virgin Islands, and Puerto Rico are sent first-class mail. Orders shipped to Canada and Mexico are sent surface mail.

International orders: Airmail—add freight equal to price of each book to the total price of order, plus $5.00 for each non-book item (audio tapes, etc.).

Surface mail—Add $1.00 per item.

Allow 4–6 weeks for delivery on all orders.
Postage and handling rates subject to change.

DISCOUNTS

We offer a 20% discount to group leaders or agents. You must order a minimum of 5 copies of the same book to get our special quantity price.

FREE CATALOG

Get a free copy of our color catalog, *New Worlds of Mind and Spirit.* Subscribe for just $10.00 in the United States and Canada ($30.00 overseas, airmail). Many bookstores carry *New Worlds*—ask for it!

Visit our web site at www.llewellyn.com for more information.

101 FENG SHUI TIPS
FOR THE HOME
Richard Webster

Now you can make subtle and inexpensive changes to your home that can literally transform your life. If you're in the market for a house, learn what to look for in room design, single level vs. split level, staircases, front door location and more. If you want to improve upon your existing home, find out how its current design may be creating negative energy, and discover simple ways to remedy the situation without the cost of major renovations or remodeling. Watch your success and spirits soar when you discover:

- How to evaluate the current feng shui energy in your home
- What to do about negative energy coming from neighbors
- How to use fountains or aquariums to attract money
- The best position for the front door
- How to arrange your living room furniture
- Colors to use and avoid for each member of the family

1-56718-809-5, 192 pp., 5 ¼ x 8, charts   **$9.95**

FENG SHUI FOR BEGINNERS
Richard Webster

Not advancing fast enough in your career? Maybe your desk is located in a "negative position." Wish you had a more peaceful family life? Hang a mirror in your dining room and watch what happens. Is money flowing out of your life rather than into it? You may want to look to the construction of your staircase!

For thousands of years, the ancient art of feng shui has helped people harness universal forces and lead lives rich in good health, wealth and happiness. The basic techniques in *Feng Shui for Beginners* are very simple, and you can put them into place immediately in your home and work environments. Gain peace of mind, a quiet confidence, and turn adversity to your advantage with feng shui remedies.

1-56718-803-6, 240 pp., 5 ¼ x 8, photos, diagrams, softcover

$12.95

FENG SHUI IN
THE GARDEN
Richard Webster

Whether you own an estate with formal gardens or live in a studio apartment with room for a some flowerpots, you can discover the remarkable benefits of using plants to create more ch'i (universal energy) in your life. Wherever you find an abundance of ch'i, the vegetation looks rich and healthy, the air smells fresh and sweet, and the water is cool and refreshing.

The ancient Chinese believed that when you live in harmony with the earth, you become a magnet for health, wealth, and happiness. *Feng Shui in the Garden* shows beginning and expert gardeners alike how to tailor their gardens to bring the greatest amount of positive energy. Select your most beneficial location, layout, flowers, colors, fragrances, herbs, and accessories based on proven feng shui principles. Discover the optimum placement of fountains, waterfalls, or swimming pools. Learn how to construct a serene secret garden, even if you live in an apartment!

ISBN: 1-56718-793-5, 5 ¼ x 8, 192 pp. $9.95